Scroll Saw
WOODEN BOWLS

Scroll Saw
WOODEN BOWLS

REVISED & EXPANDED EDITION

30
Useful & Surprisingly
Easy-to-Make Projects

CAROLE ROTHMAN

FOX CHAPEL
PUBLISHING

Acknowledgments

Many people have helped and inspired me over the years—especially the staff at Fox Chapel, the members of its scroll saw forum, and my books' readers, whose advice, support, and feedback have been immensely helpful. I'm grateful to my best friend and partner, Joe Ilardo, for his continued and invaluable support, and for the many hours he's spent editing my work; my family, whose confidence has always been a comfort; and Dave van Ess, for his wonderful design apps and utilities. Sadly, shortly before this revision was begun, the scroll saw community lost one of its most ardent enthusiasts and mentors: Hanns Derke was a long-time friend and supporter, who convinced me early on that it takes a quality saw to do quality work.

Notice about photocopying patterns

Some photocopiers and home printers may not reproduce patterns accurately. To be sure your patterns are sized correctly, a test bar like the one at the right is given with each pattern. It will measure exactly 1" when the page is printed at the percentage designated for the pattern.

TEST INCH

© 2009, 2019 by Carole Rothman and Fox Chapel Publishing Company, Inc., 903 Square Street, Mount Joy, PA 17552.

Scroll Saw Wooden Bowls, Revised & Expanded Edition (ISBN 978-1-56523-961-6) is a revised edition of *Wooden Bowls from the Scroll Saw* (ISBN 978-1-56523-433-8), published by Fox Chapel Publishing Company, Inc. This revised edition includes nine new projects. The patterns contained herein are copyrighted by the author. Readers may make copies of these patterns for personal use. The patterns themselves, however, are not to be duplicated for resale or distribution under any circumstances. Any such copying is a violation of copyright law.

All photos have been provided by the author except for the ones on pages 64, 95, and 124 (which were also used on pages 6 and 7), as well as the images used on pages 187 and 190, which are by Mike Mihalo Photography.

ISBN 978-1-56523-961-6

Library of Congress Cataloging-in-Publication Data

Names: Rothman, Carole, 1945- author.
Title: Scroll saw wooden bowls / Carole Rothman.
Other titles: Wooden bowls from the scroll saw
Description: Revised & expanded edition. | Mount Joy, PA : Fox Chapel
   Publishing Company, Inc., [2019] | Revised edition of: Wooden bowls from
   the scroll saw. 2009. | Includes index.
Identifiers: LCCN 2018059794 (print) | LCCN 2019000463 (ebook) | ISBN
   9781607656494 (ebook) | ISBN 9781565239616 (softcover)
Subjects: LCSH: Scrollwork. | Jig saws. | Woodwork--Patterns. | Bowls
   (Tableware)
Classification: LCC TT190.6 (ebook) | LCC TT190.6 .R683 2019 (print) | DDC
   684/.08--dc23
LC record available at https://lccn.loc.gov/2018059794

To learn more about the other great books from Fox Chapel Publishing, or to find a retailer near you, call toll-free
800-457-9112 or visit us at *www.FoxChapelPublishing.com*.

We are always looking for talented authors. To submit an idea, please send a brief inquiry to
acquisitions@foxchapelpublishing.com.

Printed in Singapore
First printing

Contents

Introduction: About This Edition

It's been almost ten years since the publication of Wooden Bowls from the Scroll Saw. Since that time, I've tried many new designs, profiles, and laminations, without ever losing my fascination with scrolled bowls. The variety and beauty of the objects that can be made from small pieces of wood is nothing short of astounding.

I've discovered tools, both virtual and actual, that open doors to new types of projects and to a greater level of precision. I've fine-tuned my skills and increased my appreciation of the importance of seemingly small details. The overriding goal for this revision is to share what I've learned with my readers by incorporating it, wherever relevant, into project instructions.

The publication of a new edition of this book has made it possible to add updated material in an organized and systematic manner. Chapter One, originally titled "Getting Started," has been completely revised. It now includes both basics essential for new bowl makers and material of interest to those with advanced skills.

The book retains 21 of the projects that appeared in the first edition, and has been expanded to include 9 additional ones. Some of the new projects have never been published; others have appeared in *Scroll Saw Woodworking & Crafts*. They all reflect growth and innovation that were still on the horizon when the first edition was published.

Whether you're new to making scrolled bowls or have many under your belt, you're sure to find projects you'll enjoy and challenges that will help move your work to the next level.

My ongoing love affair with scrolled bowls lies somewhere between a passion and an addiction, and I wouldn't have it any other way!

- Carole

Round Bowls

Basic Bowl and alternate, page 24

Scrolled-Top Bowl, page 36

Double-Swag Bowl, page 42

Embellish a Bowl with Plywood, page 46

Spalted Sycamore Flared-Rim Bowl, page 54

Basket Duo, page 64

Basket-Weave Bowl and alternate, page 72

Plaid Bowl, page 75

Gingham Bowl and alternate, page 78

Eight-Segment Bowl and alternate, page 112

Dizzy Bowl, page 118

Multi-Colored Twenty-Segment Bowl, page 132

Petal Bowls

Footed Candy Dish, page 170

Eight-Petal Bowl, page 32

Oval Scalloped Cypress Bowl, page 95

Four-Petal Curved Bowl, page 106

Blooming Petal Bowl, page 156

Wavy-Edged Bowls

Ripple-Edged Round Bowl, page 101

Seven-Lobe Ripple-Edged Bowl, page 136

Rectangular Bowls

Rounded-Square Bowl, page 34

Crisscross Bowl, page 82

Center Lamination Bowl, page 138

Other Bowls

Scrolled Yarn Bowl, page 88

Heart-Shaped Bowl, page 108

Open-Segmented Oval Bowl, page 124

Ginger Jar, page 164

Vases

Double-Swirl Vase, page 142

Walnut Vase, page 149

Rounded Vase with Laminated Rings, page 174

Ripple-Edged Vase, page 178

INTRODUCTION: About This Edition

CHAPTER 1

Cutting the bowls in this book requires tilting your scroll saw table. The angle is determined by width of the rings and the thickness of the stock used.

Bowl Basics

Scrolled bowls are created from concentric rings cut at an angle, then stacked, glued, and sanded to the desired shape. Making a functional and attractive three-dimensional object from a flat piece of wood is quite amazing, not to mention economical. It's also a perfect way to use up wood you have on hand. This chapter introduces the steps involved in making a scrolled bowl. Although the focus is on bowl basics—the materials, tools, and techniques you'll need to get started—I've included information that will be useful for bowl makers of any skill level who are seeking to improve the quality and variety of their work.

Attention to grain and color helps ensure an attractive bowl.

> ### Choose wood carefully
>
> Examine boards before you buy them. Wood that is cupped, twisted, or otherwise defective is usually no less expensive than perfect pieces with attractive grain.

Choosing the Wood

The first step in making a bowl is choosing the wood. The stock used for scrolled bowls typically varies in thickness from ½" (13mm) to 1" (25mm), depending on wood type and project design. Most of the projects in this book are cut from ¾" (19mm) stock, a thickness generally available wherever hardwood is sold. This thickness accommodates a variety of profiles and angles and is generally easy to cut. Thicker wood is more challenging, requiring a slower feed rate to keep the blade from deflecting and distorting the cut.

It's hard to resist the temptation to push the wood through the blade, especially if the cut is a long one, but the payoff for feeding the wood slowly is an accurately cut ring that will be far easier to work with. As you gain experience, you'll learn how to manage thick and dense wood through proper technique and careful blade selection.

Selecting the primary wood

Many types of wood are suitable for scrolled bowls, either by themselves or combined with contrasting woods. I call these "primary woods" to differentiate them from wood best used for decorative accents. Here are some primary woods that are readily available and moderately priced.

Aspen

Although more difficult to find than in past years, it is relatively inexpensive, easy to cut and shape, and when sanded well and shellacked, looks like ivory or porcelain. It is best used alone, since its softness makes it difficult to sand evenly when combined with harder wood. It is also vulnerable to discoloration from sanding dust and bleeding when combined with strongly colored woods.

Poplar

Inexpensive and easy to cut, popular is attractive when clear and light colored. Avoid pieces with large brownish-green patches, unless deliberately chosen for a special effect.

Cedar

This popular wood comes in many varieties and is easy to cut and sand. However, some types can cause respiratory problems and rashes, and others are prone to brittleness, so be sure you're familiar with the characteristics of the variety you're considering.

Mahogany

There are many types of mahogany, varying greatly in cost and beauty. All varieties are easy to cut and sand. Boards with dramatic grain, or with chatoyance (a shimmering quality), are most effective when used by themselves, with simple designs that showcase their beauty.

Maple

Either hard or soft maple is a good choice for a light-colored bowl, or for combining with a darker wood. Since color cast varies, choose your piece carefully to get the effect you want.

Cherry

A longstanding favorite of bowl makers and other woodworkers, cherry is vulnerable to burning when cut. To minimize or prevent this problem, cover the wood with clear or blue tape to lubricate the blade.

Walnut

Slightly more expensive than other common hardwoods, this attractive wood is easy to cut and sand. It also contrasts well with lighter-colored woods, such as cherry and maple.

Oak

Both white and red varieties work as stand-alone woods, or in combination with other hardwoods. Its distinctive grain pattern can produce unusual and dramatic effects when cut at an angle.

Selecting wood for combinations

Whether gluing in strips to create swags or vertical stripes, or layering wood horizontally, there are three factors to keep in mind.

Color contrast

Color contrast can be subtle, as with poplar and cedar, or dramatic, as with walnut and maple. Be aware that even boards from the same species can differ slightly in color. Walnut, for example, can vary from warm brown with a reddish cast to a cooler, brown-gray hue. These differences will become apparent as you try out different wood combinations, and can make one board a more appropriate choice than another. Since the finished color may be difficult to predict, you can preview the final results with an application of mineral spirits.

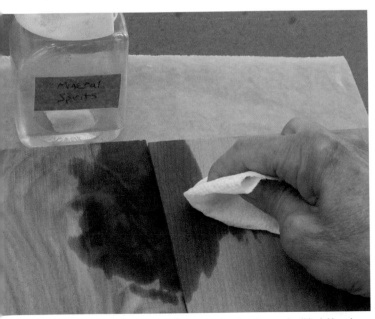

An application of mineral spirits will approximate what the wood will look like when the finish is applied.

Found Wood

Many of the bowls in this book were cut from "found" wood. I've rescued large boards of varnish-covered mahogany and teak from an old storage shed, and repurposed hard maple from my sons' baby dresser. I've even done my share of dumpster diving. However, my best discovery was a local cabinet shop whose craftsmen tossed bowl-sized cutoffs of beautiful hardwoods into bins to be used for firewood. They were pleased to find a better use for their cutoffs, and the chance to "talk shop" with experienced professionals was an unexpected bonus. Be creative with your sources. You'll benefit, and so will the environment.

Hardness

When possible, choose woods that are similar in hardness, like cherry and maple. They will be easier to sand smooth when glued together. Woods that are somewhat softer, like walnut and mahogany, can be combined successfully with slightly harder ones if care is taken to sand them evenly. Avoid great discrepancies in hardness—the beauty of the color combination will most likely be undermined by the uneven finished surface.

Sanding dust migration and color bleeding

The dust from strongly colored accent wood like padauk and redheart can migrate into the pores of adjacent pieces during sanding and discolor the wood. For this reason, it's generally not wise to pair light-colored, porous wood with strongly colored exotics. However, if your design demands that you do so, vacuuming the workpiece frequently as you sand can often remove the offending dust. Strongly colored wood can also bleed into adjacent areas if the finish is applied too generously. Minimize this likelihood by using light coats of finish. Fortunately, the discolored areas can usually be corrected with an application of the appropriate solvent, and the finish repaired.

Don't be afraid to try new woods and combinations. If you don't want to commit to a full-size project, make a small prototype to see how the wood cuts and sands. I've made my share of "designer sawdust" but have also had some wonderful discoveries—you'll never know how things will work out unless you try.

CHOOSING THE WOOD

Cutting the Rings

All the projects in this book are made from concentric rings that are cut at specific angles. These rings can be circular, but they can also be cut in a vast array of profiles, such as ovals, rectangles, and multi-lobed shapes. Beginning projects use patterns that provide cutting lines for each ring. More advanced projects, especially those with rings cut at various angles, use patterns that provide cutting lines for the first ring only; once cut, the first ring serves as the pattern for the second. The second ring serves as the pattern for the third, and the sequence continues until all rings are cut. This method requires precise cutting but gives very good alignment when the rings are stacked. Patterns are usually attached with a temporary bond (repositionable) adhesive. If your design is circular, you can bypass a paper pattern entirely and draw the rings directly on the wood with a good-quality pencil compass.

The useful awl

In this book, the awl is used for several important purposes. The first is to center patterns on the blank, which is done by inserting the point of the awl through the center of the pattern and placing it at the intersection of the guidelines. The second purpose is to create an indentation to keep the drill bit from wandering when drilling an entry hole with an angle guide. Be sure to keep your awl handy while progressing through the projects.

Marking the bowl

As you make your bowl, you'll be directed to draw pencil marks of various types on the blank or rings, including registration lines, also referred to as "guidelines." The type of pencil used can make a difference. Lines drawn with a harder lead are more precise but are lighter in color and more difficult to see. They may also score the wood if too much pressure is applied. Lines drawn with a softer lead are more visible but less precise and can leave graphite particles that penetrate the pores of soft woods like aspen. If you keep a variety of pencils on hand, you can choose the best match for each situation. For dark woods like walnut or teak, you can use a white pencil if precision is not required, as when marking glue spots or indicating ring orientation. Before gluing or sanding areas containing pencil marks, transfer any you'll still need to adjacent surfaces, then erase the originals.

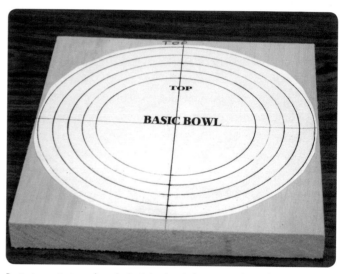

Beginning projects, such as the basic bowl, include a pattern for each ring.

More advanced projects will have a pattern for the first ring only. Each ring will then be used to create the next one.

Selecting the right blade

In the first edition of this book, I was clear in my preference for #9 Flying Dutchman blades, in reverse and ultra reverse tooth configurations. Although these are still appropriate choices, I've expanded my recommendation to include two blades made by Pegas, the Super Skip and the Modified Geometry, in the #7 size. These blades are such effective cutters that, depending on the wood, even a #5 could be used. The advantage of a smaller blade is its greater maneuverability and the option to use a smaller drill bit for the blade entry hole. I'd recommend trying the Pegas #7, in either configuration, as a starting point. Regardless of choice, be sure that the blade is tensioned fully to reduce the chance of deflection as you cut.

Table tilt and cutting direction

Most scroll saw projects are cut with the saw table perpendicular to the blade. Projects using angle cuts, such as double bevel inlay, relief cutting, and collapsible baskets, typically use small angles, no greater than 4°. To someone who has never cut at a steep angle, making accurate cuts with the saw table or arm tilted between 15° and 45° may seem nearly impossible.

If your scroll saw has a tilting table, the instructions will direct you to tilt the left or right side of the table down to a specified angle. Nearly all saws with tilting tables have a full 45° tilt to the left but vary in degree of tilt to the right. For this reason, "left side down" has become a convention, although the direction of table tilt will always be specified. If your saw has a tilting arm, just reverse the direction of the tilt given for the table. "Left side down" for tilting tables is the equivalent of "right side down" for tilting arms.

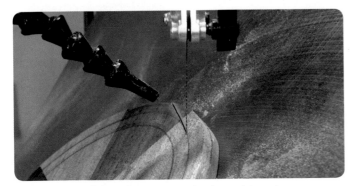

Cutting a ring in a clockwise direction means that the wood is moving counterclockwise. The cut will be wider on the upper face than on the lower one.

Blade tensioning

1. If blade slippage occurs when using higher tension, the blade ends can be lightly sanded to remove any residual oil. Clamping screws can also be sanded or filed to remove any oil, dirt, or burrs that may be contributing to the problem.

2. The blade holders on some scroll saws require considerable finger strength to tighten sufficiently to prevent slippage. This problem can be solved with an easy-to-make tightener that slips over the knob. To make this simple device, trace the outline of your scroll saw's blade-holder knob on a small block of wood, drill out the center, and cut along the outline. Be careful not to over tighten to avoid stripping threads or breaking the clamp.

This shop-made device makes it easy to tighten blade holders.

When cuts are made with blade and table perpendicular to each other, cutting direction is a matter of preference. When cuts are made at an angle, direction is critical and always clearly specified in the instructions. Nearly all cuts are made in a clockwise direction. This means that you are rotating the wood counterclockwise as it moves through the blade. In other words, the blade appears to be moving clockwise because the wood is being rotated counterclockwise. A ring cut in this manner, with the saw table tilted left side down, will have a larger diameter on the upper face than on the lower. Those few situations when counterclockwise cutting is needed are indicated clearly in boldface.

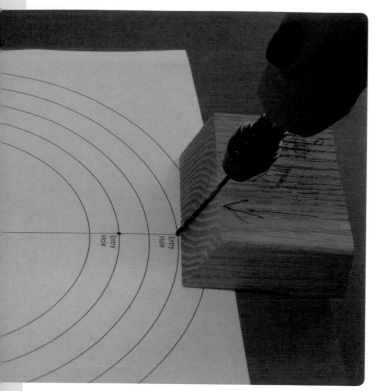

Drill holes using the smallest bit that will accommodate your blade. The smaller the hole, the easier the sanding will be later on.

Drilling blade entry holes

Cutting the outermost line of the bowl is easy—you enter the cut from the edge of the blank, then follow the pattern around until you reach your starting point. However, once that cut is made, a blade entry hole must be drilled on the next cut line so you can insert the blade and complete the ring. The angle at which this hole is drilled is usually the same as for the first cut and will be clearly specified in the instructions. The easiest way to drill the hole is with a rotary tool and shop-made angle guide. For best results, use the smallest bit that will accommodate your blade, no larger than a #54 or #56 wire size. Avoid drilling back-to-back holes on the same ring by alternating sides on successive rings, and don't be tempted to cut into the ring instead of drilling the blade entry hole. Even if you cut with the grain, vertical lines that cannot be sanded away will be left on the sides of the ring.

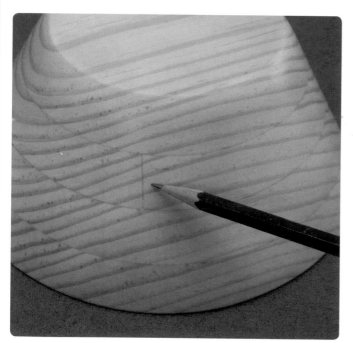

Sanding away drill marks may be tedious, but the alternative—cutting into the ring—leaves permanent cut lines on the sides of the bowl.

Making and using an angle guide

Cut a scrap of ¾" (19mm)-thick hardwood into a rectangle measuring about 2" x 1½" (51mm x 38mm). Cut one side to the desired angle and mark this angle on top for future reference. To use the guide, mark the entry hole on the pattern with an awl. Place the edge of the guide at the hole, angled edge toward the center of the bowl blank. Place the drill bit along the guide and drill through the blank. If the bit is too short to go all of the way through with the guide in place, slide the guide out of the way to complete the hole.

Having an assortment of angle guides on hand makes it easy to drill a hole at the proper angle.

Demystifying the cutting angle

Computing the cutting angle isn't magic, just trigonometry. For every combination of wood thickness and ring width, there is a cutting angle that will produce a perfect alignment when concentric rings are stacked. This angle is usually referred to as "the" cutting angle, and bowls made from rings cut at this angle have straight sides. To make curved-sided bowls, the first ring is cut at "the" cutting angle, but then the cutting angle is increased with each successive ring.

Instructions for all projects in this book provide the required cutting angles. However, these angles will only work as expected if your blank is the thickness specified in the materials list. If you want to use wood that is thicker or thinner, you will need to compute a new cutting angle. For straight-sided bowls, the angle you compute is the one you'll use for all the rings of the bowl. For curved-sided bowls, the angle you compute will be used for the first ring only, then increased with each successive ring. Computing the angle is not difficult, and on page 186 you'll find the information you need to do this. You can also go to scrollmania.com, where you'll find an app that does the computation for you once you've provided the wood thickness and ring width. This easy-to-use site, designed for makers of scrolled bowls, also contains powerful tools for creating your own bowl patterns.

The chart on page 16 gives the cutting angles for three typical ring widths, using stock that is ½" (13mm) or ¾" (19mm) thick. Cutting your rings at these angles will result in a near-perfect alignment when used to make a straight-sided bowl from a single piece of wood. If you do the computations yourself, you'll find that I've added in a small margin for error for all but the 45° cut. For example, the computed cutting angle for the combination of ⅜" (10mm) ring width and ¾" (19mm) blank thickness is 26.6°, not 28°.

A bowl with rings cut at a constant angle has sides that form a straight line.

Curved sides are created by increasing the cutting angle from ring to ring.

Patterns and project size

Every pattern in this book specifies its exact size when copied at the designated percentage. After making your copy, be certain it is sized correctly.

To change the size of a project by reducing or enlarging the pattern, you must either redraw the rings to their original width or change the cutting angle. To do so, use the formula on page 186 or the Angle Calculator that can be found at *scrollmania.com*.

I've made adjustments like these throughout the book to compensate for minor cutting deviations and imprecise angle settings on the scroll saw. These angles are sufficiently precise for a good alignment, and provide a little extra wood to compensate for miscuts. However, if you use a digital angle guide to set your saw and are confident in the precision of your cuts, you can decrease that margin and use 27°, for example, rather than 28°, for a slightly better alignment. Information on using multiple angles to produce curved sides is introduced in Chapter Four.

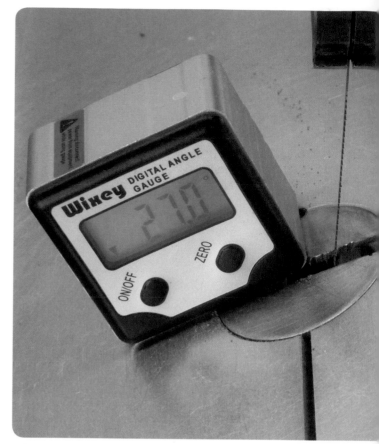

A digital angle gauge helps ensure the accuracy of your cutting angle.

Cutting angles for straight-sided bowls

Wood thickness	Ring width	Cutting angle
½" (13mm) stock	½" (13mm)	45°
½" (13mm) stock	⅜" (10mm)	38°
½" (13mm) stock	¼" (6mm)	28°
¾" (19mm) stock	½" (13mm)	34°
¾" (19mm) stock	⅜" (10mm)	28°
¾" (19mm) stock	¼" (6mm)	20°

Gluing

Once the rings are cut, they are stacked and checked for spaces between them. This can be done by shining a light behind the stacked rings or by trying to slip a thin strip of paper between them. If you can see any light, or if the paper slips in at any point, you have a space created by the rings not sitting flat against each other. Even if the blank started out flat, forces released while cutting the rings can result in a slight cupping. If not corrected, even small spaces between adjacent rings can cause unsightly glue lines. Resist the temptation to use clamping pressure to close the gaps. The likelihood that the rings can be forced completely together is small, and it takes little time to correct the problem. The best "tool" for eliminating spaces between rings, often referred to as "flattening the rings," is a full sheet of 150-grit

Evenly distributed downward pressure is essential for gluing up rings properly.

sandpaper attached to a 12" (305mm) granite floor tile with temporary bond adhesive. Don't use power sanders for this job; they are too aggressive for finesse work and can quickly ruin your bowl. Identify the areas where spaces show, and apply pressure selectively to the high spots as you rub the ring against the sandpaper. When all rings lie flat against each other, they are ready for glue-up. Remove all pencil marks from the gluing surfaces, but before doing so, relocate any that will be needed to keep the rings aligned correctly during glue-up.

Choosing a glue

It's not difficult to choose an appropriate adhesive for your bowl. Modern PVA glues meant for woodworking, such as Titebond II and III and Weldbond, are strong, non-toxic, and easy to use. I generally prefer Weldbond because it dries clear and has a quick "grab" that minimizes slippage. Titebond III is water-resistant and has a relatively long open time, but its darker color makes it more visible if the glue line is not tight.

The gluing sequence

All rings, but not the base, are usually glued together at the same time. However, for bowls with designs that require precise ring alignment, gluing the rings in stages will give better control. Once the rings are glued, they are clamped until the glue has dried. The next step is to sand the inside of the ring assembly, since sanding access will be limited once the base is attached. When this step is completed and the inside edge of the bottom ring is rounded and smooth, the base is glued into place. To remove any glue that oozes onto the surface of the base, unclamp the bowl briefly after about five minutes, scrape it off, and clean up any remaining residue with a damp paper towel. Re-clamp the bowl and let the glue dry completely. Although conventional clamps or even heavy books can be used for the glue-up, a bowl press is more convenient and helps keep the alignment while exerting strong, even pressure.

A good-quality adhesive is essential for a sound glue-up. Weldbond and Titebond II or III are appropriate choices.

Making a Bowl Press

A shop-made bowl press, with optional spacers, is invaluable to prevent slippage as you glue up your bowl rings. Though you can use other methods of clamping, a bowl press is the easiest and quickest way to exert an even amount of pressure across the bowl being clamped.

Materials

- (2) 11" (279mm) squares of ¾" (19mm) plywood
- (6) 3/8" (10mm) x 6" (152mm) carriage bolts, non-galvanized
- (6) Nuts to fit the carriage bolts, non-galvanized
- (6) Washers to fit the carriage bolts, non-galvanized
- (6) Wing nuts to fit the carriage bolts, non-galvanized
- Double -sided tape
- 1¼" (32mm) x 2½" (64mm) x 9" (229mm) piece of hardwood for spacers (optional)

Tools

- 3/8" (10mm) (press) drill bit
- 7/16" (11mm) (spacers) drill bit
- Wrench to tighten nuts

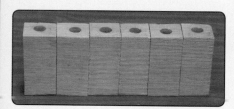

Spacers are useful accessories if you are gluing up just a few rings or a low bowl. They slide over the bolts after the top is in place, and allow you to tighten the press quickly. Use a hardwood that is at least 1" (25mm) thick, and as wide as the height you need.

Stand the wood on its side and mark six drilling holes spaced about 1½" (38mm) apart. Drill through the wood with a 7/16" (11mm) bit. Set the wood on its face and cut between the holes, forming six blocks. The spacers in the photo are about 1¼" x 1¼" x 2½" (32mm x 32mm x 64mm).

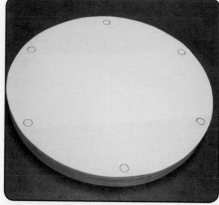

1 Cutting the plywood. Stack the plywood and attach the pieces to each other with double-sided tape. Center the pattern and cut out the circle with a scroll saw or band saw. Do not separate the circles.

2 Drilling the holes. Drill through both pieces of wood with a 3/8" (10mm) bit at the six places indicated on the pattern. Make an alignment mark on the edge of the pieces.

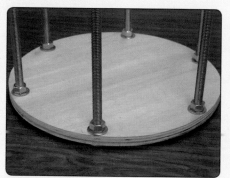

3 Completing the press. Separate the pieces. Push a carriage bolt through each hole on one of the pieces. This will be the base of your press. Place a washer and nut on top of the base and tighten the nuts evenly all around until the bolts are drawn in tightly. Enlarge the holes slightly on the second piece with a circular file or spindle sander until it fits easily over the bolts.

4 Using the press. To use the press, place a piece of wax paper on the base, place the glued-up rings on the wax paper, and place another piece of wax paper on top of the rings. Slide the top plate over the bolts. Tighten the wing nuts alternately until evenly tight. Do not over-tighten or the rings can distort.

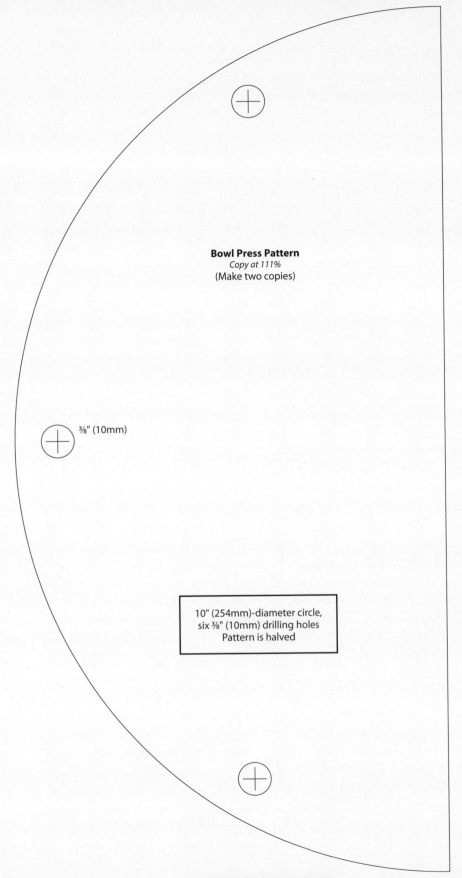

Bowl Press Pattern
Copy at 111%
(Make two copies)

⅜" (10mm)

10" (254mm)-diameter circle,
six ⅜" (10mm) drilling holes
Pattern is halved

TEST INCH

MAKING A BOWL PRESS

Sanding

Sanding is the procedure through which the rough-looking stack of rings is turned into a work of art. As with intarsia, sanding serves to shape and sculpt, as well as to smooth the surface. Preliminary shaping is done with sanders using a coarse grit, such as 80-grit. Once the shape has been established, sanding is done with progressively finer grits to refine the surface. I usually sand to 220- or 320-grit, until the surface feels smooth and ready to finish.

Sanders for bowl-making

Many different types of sanders are used for making bowls. Even if you're new to bowl-making, you're likely to own several of them. Try using the sanders you have, and add new ones when the need arises. With experience, you'll discover your preferences. Here are the sanders I used for the projects in this book, with descriptions and recommendations.

Vertical belt sander

This workshop staple is ideal for sanding the outside face of straight-sided bowls. Since it leaves vertical scratches that run across the grain, use the finest grit belt that will do the job. To sand a bowl, tilt the table to the same angle used for cutting the rings. Place the bowl bottom flat on the table. If the angle is set correctly, the side of the bowl will rest against the belt. Rotate the bowl evenly as you sand, to avoid flat spots. Sand until the surface is smooth and all blade and drill marks have been removed. If it appears that certain areas will require more sanding than others, switch to a flexible pad sander. It allows you work selectively on the problematic areas and will give a better overall result.

Spindle sander

This versatile tool is easiest to use for projects in which the spindle and table are perpendicular to each other. In this orientation, the workpiece can make contact with the spindle at any point. It's much harder to use when the table is tilted, as when sanding the inside of a straight-sided bowl. One reason is that it's more difficult to rotate the rings smoothly on a tilted table. Another is that for the rings to be sanded at the designated angle, they must contact the spindle only at the high point of the table. If the rings meet the spindle at the sides or low point of the table, the gluing surface will quickly be sanded away. For this reason, I recommend using the spindle sander for bowls with rings at least ⅜" (10mm) wide, because the ample ring width provides a small cushion in the event of mishaps. Despite the potential for disaster, when used correctly this sander creates a smooth, straight interior that's hard to match.

Flexible pad sander

These small, inexpensive sanders are ideal for sanding the outside faces of bowls, both straight- and curve-sided. Chucked into a drill press, they allow solid, two-hand control of the bowl. While you can also use these sanders for bowl interiors, you're better off using a round inflatable sander unless you're sanding a wide, shallow bowl. I find the 2" (51mm) pad the most versatile—large enough for efficient wood removal, but small enough for accurate sanding of contoured surfaces. The 3" (76mm) pad is much more aggressive; I use it for quick wood removal where maneuverability is not an issue. Sanding discs, available in plain and scalloped versions, attach easily with a hook-and-loop system that makes changing grits a snap. The standard density pad is the only type you're likely to need, although softer auxiliary pads that attach to the sander in the same way as the discs are available if you want to refine the surface without altering its shape.

Round inflatable sander

This innovative tool, referred to as "inflatable ball sander" in some projects, inflates with a small pump. It is the tool of choice for contouring the inside of bowls, especially those with flutes or petals, and is easiest to use when chucked into a drill press. Originally available only in a 2" (51mm) size, it now comes in a ¾" (19mm) version, invaluable for sanding tight areas that cannot be accessed by the larger sander. Additionally, the slits at the bottom of the small sander are more resistant to snagging than those of the larger one. Although fairly expensive, you'll find the investment worthwhile if you enjoy making bowls. Sleeves that slip over the units are available in different grits, from coarse to extra fine.

Pneumatic sanding drums

These air-filled drums are available in various lengths and widths. They are gentler alternatives to the spindle sander. I use them in widths from ¾" (19mm) to 2" (51mm), and in lengths from 1¼" (32mm) to 3¼" (83mm). As with the other inflatable sanders, I chuck them into a drill press. Sleeves, available in many grits, are easy to change and extremely durable.

Detail sanders

These small, iron-shaped sanders are useful for removing swirl marks and evening out irregularities on the outside faces of square and rectangular bowls.

Sanding mops

I use a well-worn 320-grit sanding mop to smooth the surface of bowls after the grain has been raised by a sealer coat of shellac. I also use it to buff subsequent coats, where it produces an attractive soft sheen with little effort.

Hand sanding

I usually do some hand sanding once machine-powered sanding is complete. There's invariably something in need of a touch-up—a glue spot, scratch marks, or an edge that's not quite smooth enough. I start the corrective work using 220-grit sandpaper, but if that's not sufficient I'll go to 150-grit, then sand back to the higher grit. I may even give a once-over at 320-grit if it seems needed. I've found it a good practice to set the bowl aside for several hours and then take a second look for anything that's been overlooked. Once you try this approach, you'll be impressed by how much you catch the second time around.

Applying the Finish

Before applying the finish, wipe the bowl with mineral spirits to reveal the presence of glue spots. These typically appear either as silvery lines between rings or as small shiny areas on the bowl surface. Mark these with chalk or a white pencil so you can easily find them once the mineral spirits dries. Sand them off with the finest grit that will do the job, usually 220-grit. If that's not sufficient, try 150-grit, then re-sand with 220-grit to restore the surface.

Choosing a finish

Choice of finish is a highly personal matter. Some woodworkers love oil for the way it makes the grain "pop" and for its ease of application. Others prefer a clear-coat finish that's easy to repair, like shellac, or one that forms a durable coat, like polyurethane. Still others may opt for a simple wax finish, buffed to a soft sheen. If your bowl will be in contact with food, be sure that your choice is safe for this purpose. Most finishes are considered safe once they have cured fully and the odor has dissipated, which may take as long as several weeks. For a bowl finish that's made from only food-safe ingredients, use oil made for butcher blocks or salad bowls. If you're not sure how a finish will look when applied to your bowl, test it on a scrap of the wood you are using.

Applying a shellac or lacquer finish

Although I've tried various finishes for my bowls, I find that the simplest and most versatile is shellac, brushed on or sprayed. I use it either by itself or as a base for sprayed lacquer. I start with a thin sealer coat of dewaxed shellac to seal the wood and reveal any remaining glue spots. Since the shellac raises the grain, I smooth the surface with 320-grit sandpaper, or by buffing the bowl with a small, well-worn 320-grit

sanding mop. Its small size lets me access both interior and exterior surfaces, and unlike sandpaper it leaves no particles. When I do need to remove particles, I find it easiest to use a shop vacuum and nozzle that's covered with a sock to prevent scratches. For shellac-only finishes, I apply several more coats, rubbing down the surface with 0000 steel wool after each application, if needed. If I'm using lacquer on top of the shellac, I'll usually apply a second coat of shellac, rub it down, and follow it with several coats of spray lacquer, rubbing down each coat as with the shellac. To prevent drips or sags when spraying, elevate the bowl, hold the can upright, and spray with sweeping strokes. To spray the outside of a bowl with steep sides, invert it over a spray can or other tall, stable object.

It's now time to move on to Chapter 2, which starts with a step-by-step guide to the creation of the Basic Bowl.

CHAPTER 9

The bowls in this chapter are created by a series of angled rings that are stacked, glued together, and sanded.

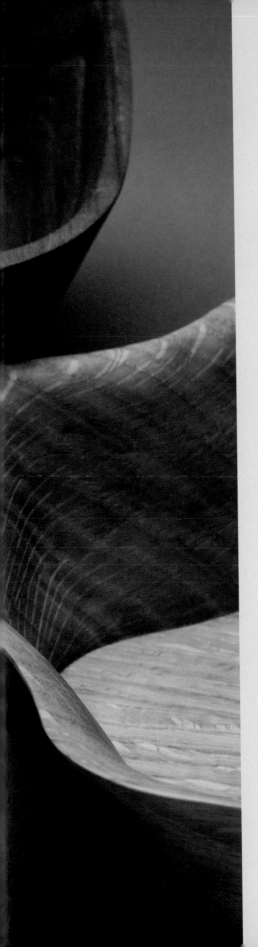

Basic Stacked Bowls

All of the projects in this book consist of a series of rings, cut at an angle, glued up, and sanded. Even vases are just several series of rings. This means that the techniques and principles used are essentially the same whether your project is simple or complex. The difficulty of your project depends upon several factors: choice of wood, cutting angles, bowl shape, and whether lamination is used.

The projects in this chapter introduce two different methods to guide your cuts: the pattern method and the ring method. The pattern method uses a paper pattern consisting of an outline and a series of two to five concentric rings. Having a pattern for each ring helps maintain the shape of the bowl, but doesn't allow adjustment for slight cutting irregularities. The first three bowls in this chapter use the pattern method.

The ring method uses a paper pattern consisting of an outline and first ring only. Each ring, when cut, forms the pattern for the next, resulting in a more precise alignment than possible with the pattern method. Since the shape of each ring depends on the one cut before it, accurate cutting is critical. The ring method must be used with bowls requiring cutting of multiple angles or that require inserts of contrasting wood, but it can be used with any bowl. The last bowl in this chapter, the Scrolled-Top Bowl, introduces the ring method.

The chapter starts with a step-by-step construction of a basic round bowl, and will familiarize you with basic techniques. Once you're comfortable with the basics, you can try other shapes and learn how to add interest and variety to your work.

Basic Bowl: A Step-by-Step Guide

The first bowl I ever made was cut from aspen. Aspen is soft and inexpensive, which makes it a low-risk choice for a first bowl. If you've never worked with aspen, you'll be surprised at how attractive it is when sanded well and shellacked.

Wood
- 8" x 8" x ¾" (203mm x 203mm x 19mm) aspen or other wood that is easy to cut

Materials
- Packing tape (optional)
- Glue
- Repositionable adhesive
- Sanding discs for flexible pad sander, assorted grits 60 to 400
- Sandpaper for inflatable ball sander, assorted grits 60 to 320 (optional)
- Sandpaper for hand sanding, assorted grits 220 to 400
- 0000 steel wool or 320-grit sanding sponge
- Spray shellac

Tools
- Scroll saw blade, size #9
- Drill bit size #54 or ⅟₁₆" (2mm)
- Awl
- Ruler
- Bowl press or clamps
- 2" (51mm) flexible pad sander
- Inflatable ball sander and pump (optional)

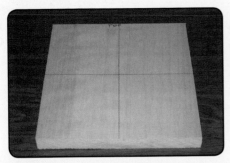

1 Drawing the guidelines. Draw two intersecting lines through the middle of the bowl blank. These form guidelines that help you align the rings properly when gluing up the bowl. Mark the top of the blank.

2 Aligning the pattern. Make a copy of the pattern from page 29. Apply the repositionable adhesive. Puncture the middle point of the pattern with an awl, and place the point of the awl at the intersection of the two lines on the wood. Line up the guidelines on the pattern with the guidelines on the wood and press the pattern into place.

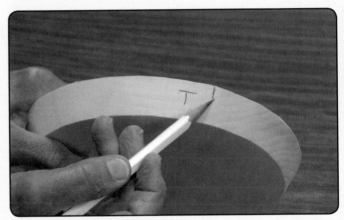

To tape or not to tape

Many scrollers use packing tape over or under patterns, or blue painter's tape under patterns, to lubricate the blade while cutting. I've found that certain hardwoods, like cherry, are much more likely to burn without tape, while softer woods, like mahogany, do fine without it. If you're not sure what to do, try a test cut to see if it's worth the extra step.

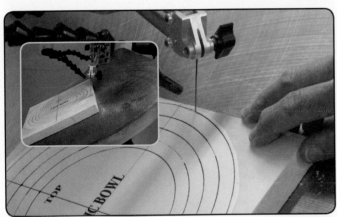

3 Cutting the outline. Tilt the table of your scroll saw to 28°, left side down. Use a #9 blade, tensioned tightly, to cut clockwise along the outmost line. Let the blade cut freely to avoid distortion and keep the proper angle. Remove bowl from waste.

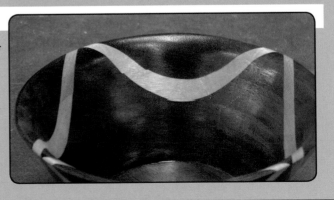

4 Marking the top. Mark the top of the bowl on the outer face of the blank. This will help keep the rings oriented when you glue them up. Extend each of the four guidelines onto the outer face of the blank.

Guidelines

It's important to draw guidelines and other orienting marks to maintain alignment. Proper alignment of grain makes the bowl look as though it were constructed from a single piece of wood, and gives the illusion of continuity to laminations. Sometimes misalignments are barely noticeable. Unfortunately, that was not true of this mahogany swag bowl.

BASIC BOWL: A STEP-BY-STEP GUIDE

CHAPTER 2: Basic Stacked Bowls

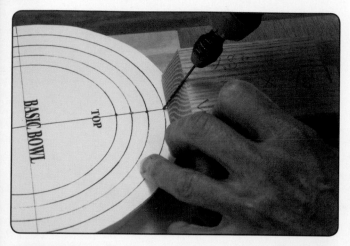

5 **Drilling the entry holes.** If using a hand drill or rotary tool, mark all entry holes with an awl to prevent the bit from slipping. Place a 28° angle guide so it faces the center of the blank. Drill all entry holes with a #54 or 1/16" (2mm) bit.

Alternative for drilling entry holes

If you don't have the correct angle guide at hand, you can use the scrap from your first cut as an angle guide. Or, if you have a drill press with a tilting table, you can set the table to 28° and drill the entry holes, angling them toward the center of the blank.

6 **Completing the first ring.** Insert the blade through the outermost hole and cut clockwise along the pattern line to complete the first ring. Place the ring on top of the remainder of the bowl blank. Transfer the guidelines from the pattern to the inside face of the cut ring. Extend guidelines from the top of the ring onto the inner and outer edges.

7 **Cutting the second, third, and fourth rings.** Insert the blade through the next entry hole and cut out the second ring as in Step 6. Mark the top and extend all guidelines. Repeat for the third and fourth rings. Each should line up with the previous ring.

8 **Stacking the rings.** Stack the rings, keeping the tops oriented, and match up the guideline extensions. Extend the marks from ring to ring on both the inside and outside surfaces so you can re-align them easily.

9 **Preparing for gluing.** Erase all guidelines on the top face of the rings to prevent them from appearing as tiny dots on the sides of the bowl. Stack the rings and hold the stacked bowl up to the light. Look for spaces between rings. If you find any, sand the ring faces smooth until the spaces disappear.

Testing and adjusting the angle

Every project in this book includes recommended cutting angles. These angles are based on two factors: thickness of the wood and width of the ring. Wood that is thicker or thinner than specified or a table tilt that is "off" will result in rings not lining up as well as they should. Before cutting any bowl, you might want to test the suggested cutting angle, using wood the same thickness as your bowl, to be sure it works for you. Follow the steps below to make an angle tester and test the angle.

If your cut was not accurate, try a tighter blade tension and take extra care not to distort the blade while cutting.

If your cutting angle was accurate and the ring hangs over the edge of the base by more than a small amount, increase the table angle by one or two degrees. If the ring sits inside the base by more than a small amount, reduce the table angle by one or two degrees. To counter the forces of gravity when cutting at a steep angle, be sure to keep the wood pushed up against the blade.

1 **Cutting the test ring.** Draw a 3" (76mm) circle with one ring the same width as your bowl's rings. Cut the ring as though it were a bowl.

2 **Checking the alignment.** Place the ring on top of the base and see how well it lines up. If your angle is correct, the two pieces should be closely aligned.

3 **Checking the angle of the cut.** If the pieces are not well aligned, check to see if your ring was cut at the intended angle. Do this by holding the ring next to the blade and see if the two line up.

10 **Gluing the rings.** Set the base aside. It will be glued on in Step 13. Stack the rings and do a final check for alignment. Starting with the smallest ring, dot the top of the ring with glue. Spread the glue, covering surfaces thoroughly. Press the next ring firmly into place. Check alignment and adjust rings if necessary. Repeat for the remaining rings.

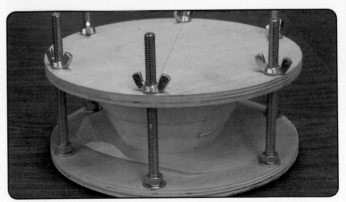

11 **Using the bowl press.** Place the glued-up rings in the bowl press, using wax paper above and below the rings. Tighten the wing nuts alternately, as you would on a car wheel, exerting firm but not excessive pressure. Let dry for a few minutes, unclamp, and clean up any glue squeeze-out. Re-clamp and let dry thoroughly.

BASIC BOWL: A STEP-BY-STEP GUIDE

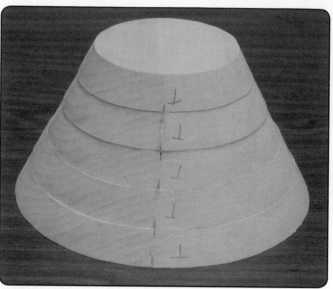

12 **Sanding the bowl interior.** Use a spindle sander with the table set to 28°. Be sure the bowl contacts the spindle only at this angle. You can also use an inflatable ball or flexible pad sander. Be sure the inside of the bottom ring is round—it cannot be corrected after attaching the base. The bottom of the smallest ring should be at least ¼" (6mm) wide for gluing to the base.

13 **Gluing on the base.** Sand the top of the base smooth and glue it to the bottom ring using the bowl press. Let it sit for about five minutes, then remove it from the press and clean excess glue from the inside bottom surface as thoroughly as possible. Return to press, and let dry.

14 **Sanding the outside.** Use a vertical belt sander or flexible pad sander to sand off all irregularities. Use progressively finer grits until the bowl is smooth. Re-sand inner surfaces if necessary. Try to keep the width of the top rim even. Round off the edges of the top ring and base.

15 **Applying the finish.** Apply mineral spirits to the bowl to reveal glue spots. Mark any with a white pencil or chalk. When the bowl is dry, sand off the glue spots. Apply the first coat of shellac and let dry. Smooth the surface with a 320-grit sanding sponge or 0000 steel wool. Vacuum, wipe with a damp cloth or paper towel, then recoat. Repeat until desired finish is obtained.

Alternate version

To make the alternate version of the basic bowl, you will need to make the following changes to the materials and instructions:

- Wood is ½" (13mm) zebrawood, not ¾" (19mm) aspen

- Outer circle is 7¼" (184mm), not 7" (178mm)

- Cutting angle is 38°, not 28°

- Base is inverted and thinned to about ¼" (6mm)

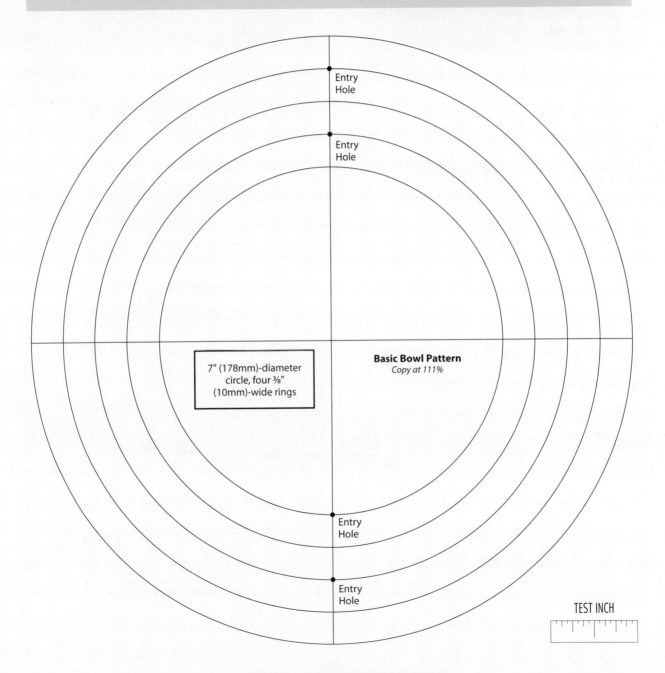

Entry Hole

Entry Hole

7" (178mm)-diameter circle, four ⅜" (10mm)-wide rings

Basic Bowl Pattern
Copy at 111%

Entry Hole

Entry Hole

TEST INCH

BASIC BOWL: A STEP-BY-STEP GUIDE

Creating contour with freehand sanding

Freehand sanding serves a number of different purposes. At its most basic, it lets you achieve a smooth and even finish. As a technique for shaping, it mimics the effect of cutting tools on lathe-turned bowls by removing wood selectively to create interesting angles and curves. Bowl sanders can be used with a drill, drill press, or flexible shaft. I prefer using a drill press since it leaves my hands free to rotate the bowl. Much sawdust will be generated, so be sure to wear a dust mask, use eye protection, and vacuum your work and work area frequently.

If you've never done freehand sanding, it may take a while to feel comfortable with the equipment. If you use a light touch and check your work frequently, you're not likely to create a problem you can't correct. Proper technique depends on whether you are sanding the inside or outside of the bowl, and whether you are shaping aggressively or trying to achieve a smooth, even finish.

In general, it is important to hold the bowl tightly, move it against the direction of rotation of the sander, and keep light but even pressure. Unless you've already done a preliminary straight sanding, start with a coarse grit for shaping, and move to progressively finer ones to achieve a smooth finish. The coarser the grit is, the more pronounced the sanding marks will be—try starting with 100 grit, moving to 80 or 60 only if you need more cutting power. Once the bowl is shaped, use a light touch to avoid distortion. For ease of access, most inside sanding is done before gluing on the bottom; be careful not to catch the sander on the lower edge. Be aware of the contour you are trying to achieve, and check your work frequently.

Inner surfaces

Inflatable ball sanders are invaluable for sanding petals, flutes, and reaching lower rings in tall bowls. They can also be used on flat surfaces if you keep the work moving to avoid creating ridges. Short brushing strokes work well to smooth the sides.

Flexible pad sanders can be used on all but the narrowest parts of bowl interiors. The 2" (51mm) size with a pad of standard density is the most versatile, but a 1½" (38mm) pad may be needed to sand areas with small diameters. Short, light strokes help maintain control.

Shaping a lip with an outward flare

To shape an outward flare, hold the bowl securely with both hands and use short inside-to-outside strokes against the upper edge. Be careful to avoid distortion once the desired shape is achieved. Hand sanding will smooth out minor irregularities.

Use inflatable ball sanders to sand interiors.

Use inside-to-outside strokes to shape the lip's outward flare.

Contouring the base

Use a 2" (51mm) flexible pad sander to smooth and shape the outside, stroking the bowl lightly to avoid ridges. Once the base is attached, it can be contoured by holding the bowl upside-down and sanding away material at the lower edge until the desired shape is achieved.

The base can be contoured after being glued to the bowl.

A beginner makes a bowl

To make sure my instructions for the basic bowl were easy to follow, I asked a novice scroller to construct a bowl and indicate where instructions were not clear.

His glued-up bowl looked a little rough, but once sanded and finished was quite impressive.

BASIC BOWL: A STEP-BY-STEP GUIDE

Eight-Petal Bowl

Petal-shaped bowls of various configurations are found throughout this book. An inflatable ball sander is highly recommended for bowls of this type to keep the flutes nicely shaped and even. If you don't have one, a flexible pad sander in the 1½" (38mm) size can be used for the bowl insides. Since a great deal of shaping is involved, save the denser woods for other projects and use an easy-to-sand wood like mahogany or walnut. Take your time when sanding the bowl and check the shape frequently to be sure the petals remain equal in size.

Wood

- (1) 8" x 8" x ¾" (203mm x 203mm x 19mm) walnut or other wood that is easy to cut and sand

Materials

- Packing tape (optional)
- Glue
- Repositionable adhesive
- Sanding discs for flexible pad sander, assorted grits 60 to 400
- Sandpaper for inflatable ball sander, assorted grits 60 to 320 (optional)
- Sandpaper for hand sanding, assorted grits 220 to 400
- 0000 steel wool or 320-grit sanding sponge
- Spray shellac or Danish oil

Tools

- Scroll saw blade, size #9
- Drill bit size #54 or 1/16" (2mm)
- Awl
- Ruler
- Bowl press or clamps
- 2" (51mm) flexible pad sander
- Inflatable ball sander and pump (optional) or 1½" (38mm) flexible pad sander

MAKING THE BOWL

1. Draw guidelines on the bowl blank.
2. Attach the pattern with repositionable adhesive.
3. Tilt the table 28°, left side down.
4. Cut the bowl outline in a clockwise direction.
5. Mark the top of the outer rim.
6. Drill 28° entry holes and cut out three rings.
7. Mark the top and draw guidelines on each ring.

8. Stack the rings. Check for alignment and spaces.
9. Glue the rings, clamp them, and let dry.
10. Sand the inside of the bowl smooth.
11. Glue on the base, clamp, and let dry.
12. Shape the outside of bowl.
13. Apply finish of choice.

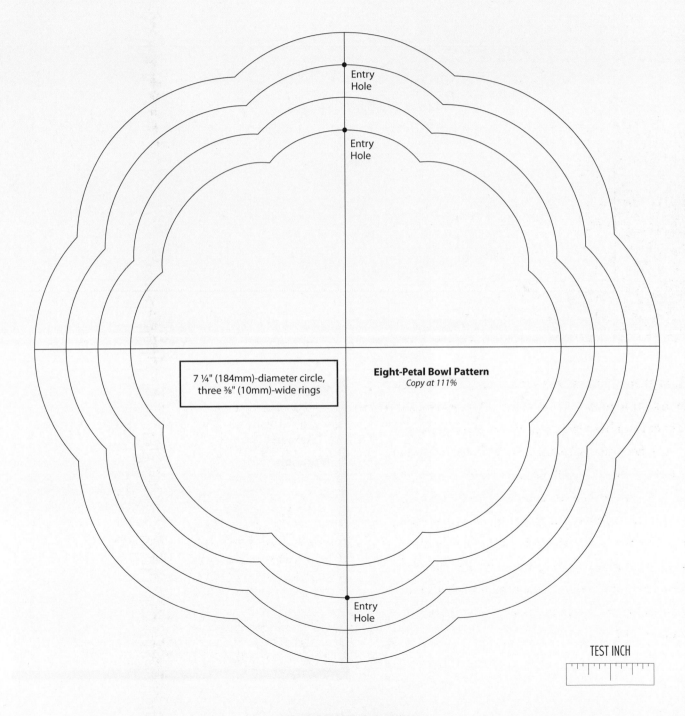

Entry Hole

Entry Hole

Entry Hole

7 ¼" (184mm)-diameter circle, three ⅜" (10mm)-wide rings

Eight-Petal Bowl Pattern
Copy at 111%

TEST INCH

EIGHT-PETAL BOWL

Rounded-Square Bowl

The rounded square is a practical and useful shape for a bowl. Its uncluttered lines also make it the perfect showcase for a special piece of wood. I decided to use a piece of teak I had rescued from a storage shed. Despite teak's reputation for being hard to glue and finish because of its high oil content, I had no problem treating it as any other wood. However, its high silica content (which gives it a non-skid quality for decking) makes it highly abrasive, so if you use teak, be prepared to change blades frequently.

Wood
- (1) 8" x 8" x ¾" (203mm x 203mm x 19mm) teak or wood of choice

Materials
- Packing tape (optional)
- Glue
- Repositionable adhesive
- Sanding discs for flexible pad sander, assorted grits 60 to 400
- Sandpaper for inflatable ball sander, assorted grits 60 to 320 (optional)
- Sandpaper for hand sanding, assorted grits 220 to 400
- 0000 steel wool or 320-grit sanding sponge
- Spray shellac or Danish oil

Tools
- Scroll saw blade, size #9
- Drill bit size #54 or 1/16" (2mm)
- Awl
- Ruler
- Bowl press or clamps
- 2" (51mm) flexible pad sander
- Inflatable ball sander and pump (optional)

MAKING THE BOWL

1. Draw guidelines on the bowl blank.
2. Attach the pattern.
3. Tilt the table 28°, left side down.
4. Cut the bowl outline in a clockwise direction.
5. Mark the top of the outer rim.
6. Drill 28° entry holes and cut out three rings.
7. Mark the top and draw guidelines on each ring.

8. Stack the rings. Check for alignment and spaces.
9. Glue the rings, clamp them, and let dry.
10. Sand the inside of the bowl smooth.
11. Glue on the base, clamp, and let dry.
12. Shape the outside of bowl.
13. Apply finish of choice.

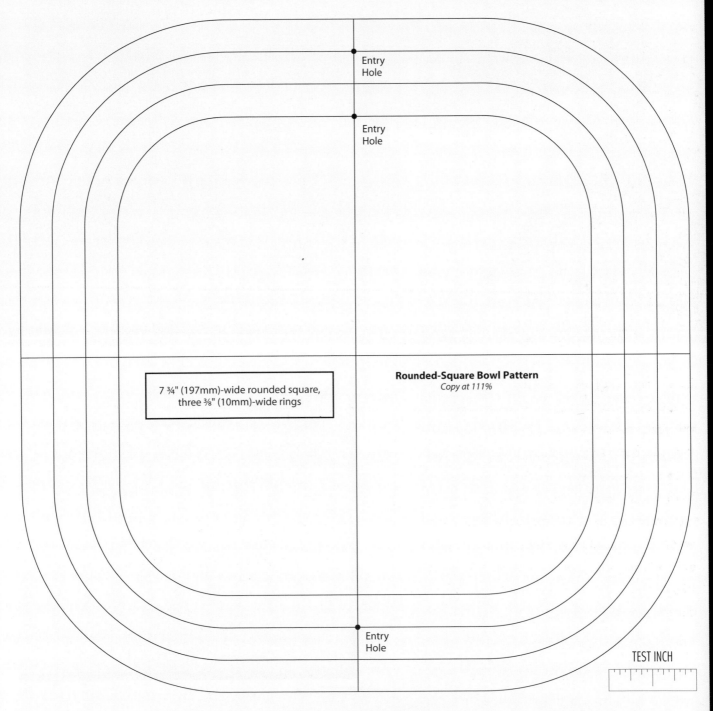

Entry Hole

Entry Hole

7 ¾" (197mm)-wide rounded square, three ⅜" (10mm)-wide rings

Rounded-Square Bowl Pattern
Copy at 111%

Entry Hole

TEST INCH

ROUNDED-SQUARE BOWL

Scrolled-Top Bowl

I decided to end this chapter with a bowl that could not be more different from the Basic Bowl. It highlights how much variety can be obtained from the basic round pattern. I modeled this project after a lathe-turned bowl I bought several years ago at a crafts show. The free-form edge is cut after the bowl is completed, and the base is sharply contoured by sanding. To obtain the desired effect, the bowl must be sufficiently tall to allow for cutting the curve, and the sides must be of uniform thickness.

Wood

- (1) 8" x 8" x ¾" (203mm x 203mm x 19mm) maple or wood of your choice

Materials

- Packing tape (optional)
- Glue
- Repositionable adhesive
- Sanding discs for flexible pad sander, assorted grits 60 to 400
- Sandpaper for inflatable ball sander, assorted grits 60 to 320 (optional)
- Sandpaper for hand sanding (220 to 400)
- 0000 steel wool or 320-grit sanding sponge
- Spray shellac or Danish oil

Tools

- Scroll saw blade, size #9
- Spiral blade #3 (optional)
- Drill bit size #54 or 1/16" (2mm)
- Awl
- Ruler
- Bowl press or clamps
- 2" (51mm) flexible pad sander
- Inflatable ball sander and pump (optional)

Because the ¼" (6mm)-wide rings that are needed don't allow much extra wood for correcting irregularities, an alternative cutting approach, the ring method, is used. This method, where each ring is used as the model for the one that follows it, produces a more precise alignment than the pattern method. Patterns for bowls cut with the ring method consist of an outline and cutting guide for the first ring. The following instructions are for a five-ring bowl cut at a 20° angle, but the procedure is the same regardless of the number of rings or cutting angle. The ring method is used in later chapters for bowls with inserts of different colored woods, and for bowls requiring more than one cutting angle.

MAKING THE BOWL

1. Draw guidelines on the blank and attach the pattern with repositionable adhesive.

2. Cut the first ring with the saw table tilted at 20°, left side down, cutting the outline in a clockwise direction.

3. Drill a 20° entry hole and complete the first ring. Remove the pattern.

4. Place the ring on top of the blank, keeping guidelines aligned, and transfer the guidelines from the blank to the ring. Keeping the ring in place, trace the inside of the ring on the bowl blank to form the pattern for the second ring (see photo, right). Mark the top of the ring.

5. Drill a 20° entry hole for the second ring and cut out the second ring at a 20° angle, table tilted left side down, cutting clockwise.

6. Cut the remaining three rings in the same way, transferring guidelines to each ring as it is cut. There will be five rings when you are done.

7. Stack the rings. Check for alignment and spaces.

8. Glue the rings, clamp them, and let dry.

9. Sand the inside of the bowl smooth.

10. Glue on the base, clamp, and let dry.

11. Shape the outside of the bowl, contouring the base steeply.

12. Attach the top pattern to the inside of the bowl with adhesive. You will probably need to make some adjustments to achieve a good fit.

4 **Trace the inside** of the ring on the blank.

13. Begin cutting at the top of the bowl. Rotate the bowl to get as much clearance as possible (see photo, right).

14. When you can cut no further, back out and cut off the waste, cutting from the top of the bowl inward. Continue cutting, removing waste to permit access (see photo below). Work your way around the bowl in this manner until you can resume cutting normally. If you cannot cut as deeply as needed with a regular blade, deepen the cut with a spindle sander, or use a spiral blade.

15. When the cut is complete, sand the edge smooth.

16. Apply finish of choice.

Cutting

For rings to align perfectly, the bottom of the first ring must match the top of the second ring, and so on. Using each ring as the pattern for the next usually gives a more precise alignment than using a paper pattern. However, if any ring is substantially miscut, all that follow will be misshapen. To prevent this from happening, check the shape of each ring after it is cut, and make corrections in the outline of the next ring if necessary.

13 Scroll the edge.

14 Cut off the waste if needed.

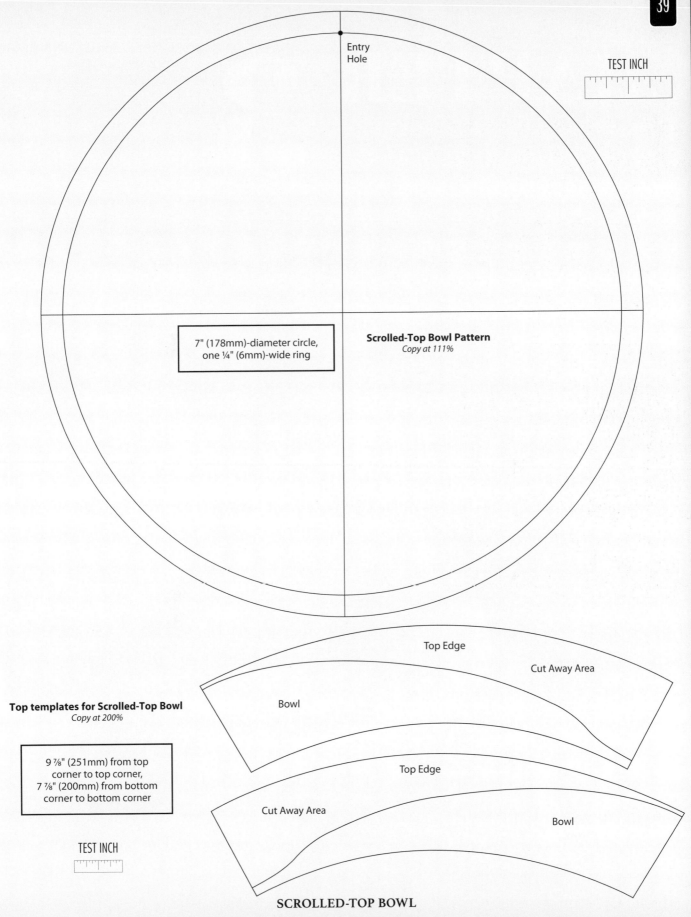

Entry
Hole

TEST INCH

7" (178mm)-diameter circle,
one ¼" (6mm)-wide ring

Scrolled-Top Bowl Pattern
Copy at 111%

Top Edge

Cut Away Area

Bowl

Top templates for Scrolled-Top Bowl
Copy at 200%

9 ⅞" (251mm) from top
corner to top corner,
7 ⅞" (200mm) from bottom
corner to bottom corner

Top Edge

Cut Away Area

Bowl

TEST INCH

SCROLLED-TOP BOWL

CHAPTER 3

The bowls in this chapter were created by gluing up stock to produce a bowl blank with multiple woods.

Laminated Wood Bowls

Creating a laminated wood bowl with the scroll saw is an exciting process—swags, curves, and interesting patterns of various kinds emerge unexpectedly when flat pieces of wood are cut into concentric rings. There are two different ways to create a lamination. The first is by gluing up stock in various configurations to produce a bowl blank that consists of two or more different woods. The second is by using a plain blank and inserting contrasting rings during the bowl-cutting process. These methods can be used separately or combined.

Although the cutting and gluing process for making laminated bowls is similar to that used for single-wood bowls, there are two main differences.

First, because of the sanding that may be needed to remove glue and irregularities from the finished blank, you may end up with a blank that is slightly thinner than required. For some glue-ups, the easiest way to avoid this problem is to start with wood slightly thicker than specified, then sand to the correct thickness. If this is not feasible, and your completed blank is too thin, you can easily compute a new cutting angle to compensate, using the instructions on page 186. Re-computing the cutting angle will also compensate for excessive thickness in the event you are not able to correct it by sanding.

Second, while careful alignment during glue-up is always important, laminations involving glued-in strips must be aligned even more precisely to maintain the continuity of the pattern between adjacent rings.

The bowls in this chapter provide a sampling of different types of laminations. Besides being fun and challenging, they are a good way to use up scraps of wood you can't bear to throw away.

Double-Swag Bowl: A Step-by-Step Guide

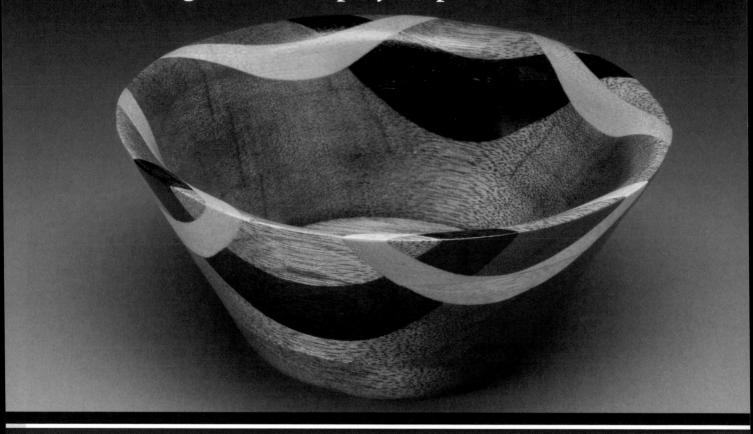

Intersecting swags of different colors add elegance to this simple round bowl. The step-by-step instructions will guide you through the multi-step lamination. Once the bowl blank is glued up and sanded, the bowl is completed like a single-wood bowl.

Wood
- (1) 8" x 8" x ¾" (203mm x 203mm x 19mm) maple or wood of your choice

Materials
- Packing tape (optional)
- Glue
- Repositionable adhesive
- Sanding discs for flexible pad sander, assorted grits 60 to 400
- Sandpaper for inflatable ball sander, assorted grits 60 to 320 (optional)
- Sandpaper for hand sanding (220 to 400)
- 0000 steel wool or 320-grit sanding sponge
- Spray shellac or Danish oil

Tools
- Scroll saw blade, size #9
- Spiral blade #3 (optional)
- Drill bit size #54 or 1/16" (2mm)
- Awl
- Ruler
- Bowl press or clamps
- 2" (51mm) flexible pad sander
- Inflatable ball sander and pump (optional)

LAMINATION GUIDE

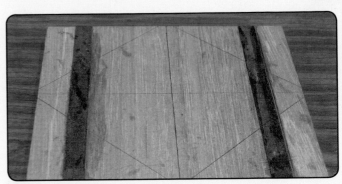

1 Attach the mahogany and purpleheart. Glue up the three pieces of mahogany and two pieces of purpleheart in this order: ¾" (19mm) mahogany, purpleheart, 4½" (114mm) mahogany, purpleheart, ¾" (19mm) mahogany. Clamp and let dry overnight. Trim, if necessary, to form a 7" (178mm) square.

2 Divide the blank. Draw intersecting guidelines across the blank. The center point should be 3½" (89mm) from each side. Make a mark ¼" (6mm) on each side of the end points of the guidelines. You will have eight marks. Connect the marks as shown to form corner triangles.

3 Attach the yellowheart. Cut off the triangles, marking each triangle and its adjacent side so you can reposition it properly. Sand all of the cut sides flat. Glue two pieces of yellowheart on opposite sides of the blank, ¼" (6mm) side up. The strips should sit flat against the blank. Clamp, using pieces of wood to avoid damaging the sides, and let dry. Glue the remaining pieces of yellowheart in the same manner.

4 Attach the corners. Glue two opposite corners onto the corresponding sides of the blank. Clamp and let dry. Use a straight edge to be sure the purpleheart strips are aligned properly, and be careful the pieces don't shift. Glue the remaining two corners in the same manner.

Drawing a pattern directly on wood

To guarantee precise pattern placement on a complex lamination, circular patterns can easily be drawn directly on the bowl blank. Here's how:

Draw guidelines on the bowl blank, centering them on the lamination. Measuring from the center point, mark a point on one of the guidelines that is half the bowl's diameter. Position the point of your compass at the intersection of the guidelines and draw a circle the same as the diameter of your bowl. Using the same center point, draw a second circle inside the first so that the distance between the two circles is the same as the width of the ring you will be cutting.

5 Sand the blank. Use a sanding drum or hand sander to sand the blank smooth. Redraw the guidelines if they have been sanded away.

MAKING THE BOWL

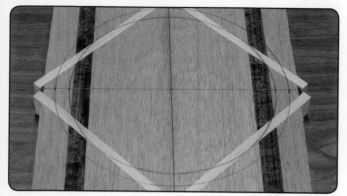

1 Drawing the outline and first ring. Mark a point on one of the guidelines that is 3¼" (83mm) from the center of the circle. Use your compass and that mark to draw a circle 6½" (165mm) in diameter. Mark a point on one of the guidelines that is ⅜" (10mm) inside this circle. Use your compass to draw a smaller circle that forms the inside edge of the first ring.

2 Cutting the first ring. Tilt the scroll saw table to an angle of 28°, left side down. Using a #9 blade, cut clockwise along the outer circle. Mark the top on the outside of the ring and extend guidelines down the sides.

3 Finishing the first ring. Use an angle guide or drill press with a tilting table to drill a 28° entry hole on the inner ring with a #54 or 1/16" (2mm) drill bit, pointed toward the center of the blank. Insert the blade through the entry hole and cut on the inner line to complete the first ring.

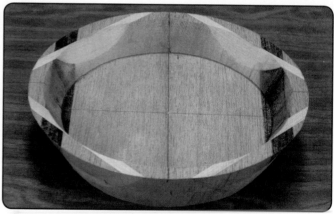

4 Marking and cutting the second ring. Place the ring you just cut on the bowl blank and align using the guidelines. Mark the top. Transfer the guidelines from the blank to the lower edge of the first ring. Keeping marks aligned, use the inside edge of the first ring to mark the cutting line for the second ring. Use the angle guide to drill an entry hole for the second ring directly opposite the top. (Alternating top and bottom makes the drill marks easier to sand out than if they were positioned directly behind each other.) Cut and mark the second ring. Use the second ring to draw the cutting line for the third ring.

5 Cutting the third ring. Cut and mark the third ring in the same way as the second.

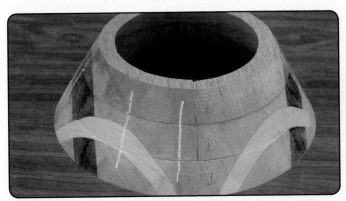

6 Preparing rings for gluing. Make sure all guidelines have been transferred to the sides of the rings. Erase any marks on the tops and lower edges of the rings. Stack and align the rings carefully. Draw lines down the side with a white pencil to help keep the alignment when gluing up. Check for spaces between the rings and sand flat if necessary.

7 Gluing the rings. Set aside the base. It will be glued on in Step 9. Place dots of glue on the top of the third ring. Spread the glue evenly, covering the surface completely. Place the second ring on top, aligning carefully. Repeat the process for the first ring. Clamp the bowl with wax paper above and below the rings. After a few minutes, unclamp the bowl briefly and remove excess glue. Re-clamp and let dry.

8 Sanding the inside. Using a flexible pad sander or inflatable ball, sand the inside of the bowl. These tools give more flexibility for shaping than a spindle sander. Use progressively finer grits to sand the inside of the bowl smooth. Do a preliminary sanding of the outside with the flexible pad sander.

9 Gluing on the base. Align the base and glue it to the underside of the rings. Clamp the bowl. After a few minutes clean off glue residue on the inside of bowl. Re-clamp the bowl and let it dry.

10 Sanding and shaping the outside and upper edge. Use the flexible pad sander to complete the sanding of the bowl, going from coarser to finer grits. Shape the lower edge and sand an outward flare on the upper edge to accentuate the swag. Check the bowl for shape and smoothness as you sand.

11 Finishing the bowl. Apply mineral spirits to the bowl to reveal any glue spots. Mark with a white pencil or chalk. When dry, sand off the glue spots. Apply the first coat of shellac and let it dry. Smooth the surface with a 320-grit sanding sponge or 0000 steel wool. Vacuum, remove the remaining particles with a damp cloth or paper towel, then recoat. Repeat until desired finish is obtained.

DOUBLE-SWAG BOWL: A STEP-BY-STEP GUIDE

Embellish a Bowl with Plywood: A Step-by-Step Guide

Looking for new ideas for scrolled bowls, I came upon some attractive projects made from laminated blocks of plywood. Impressed by the economy of this approach and its unusual beauty, I created a bowl that features a center accent ring made of plywood embellished with contrasting pieces of veneer. The round shape, generous ring width, and construction shortcuts make this bowl ideal for anyone looking to make something different, but not extremely difficult or time consuming.

Wood

- Mahogany, ¾" (19mm) thick: 2 each 7½" x 7½" (191mm x 191mm)
- Mahogany, ¼" (6mm) thick: 7½" x 7½" (191mm x 191mm)
- Maple veneer, ¹⁄₁₆" (2mm) thick: 3 each 7½" x 7½" (191mm x 191mm)
- Wood of choice, ¾" (19mm): accent ring guide, 6" x 6" (152mm x 152mm)
- Plywood, void free, ¾" (19mm) thick: accent ring short sides, 4 each ¾" x 3" (19mm x 76mm); accent ring long sides, 4 each, ¾" x 5" (19mm x 127mm)

Materials

- Spray adhesive: repositionable
- Sandpaper
- Wood glue, such as Weldbond

- Steel wool: 0000 grit
- Spray shellac
- Spray lacquer

Tools

- Scroll saw blades: #2, #9
- Awl
- Drill with bits: #54 wire size or ¹⁄₁₆" (2mm) dia.
- Angle guides, shop made: 28° and 35°(see Tip)
- Bowl press or clamps and boards for gluing
- Round inflatable sander and sleeves: assorted grits
- Flexible pad sander, 2" (51mm)-dia., with assorted sanding discs
- White pencil

MAKING THE ACCENT RING

1 **Cut and mark the octagon.** Attach the octagonal pattern to the accent-ring blank using repositionable adhesive. Cut the perimeter only of the octagon. Mark the center with an awl, remove the pattern, and copy the numbers from the pattern to the face of the wood near the edges of the wedges.

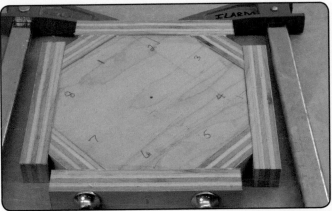

3 **Attach the long plywood strips.** Glue and clamp 5" (127mm)-long plywood strips to segments 2 and 6. Repeat for segments 4 and 8. Sand the upper and lower faces of the piece until the plywood strips are smooth and even.

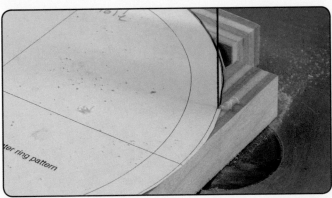

4 **Cut the accent ring.** Attach the accent-ring pattern to the sanded piece using repositionable adhesive. Use the awl to align the center of the pattern with the mark made in Step 1. Cut along the outer circle of the pattern. Carefully remove the pattern and save it for Step 6.

2 **Attach and trim the short plywood strips.** Glue and clamp two 3" (76mm)-long strips to segments 1 and 5 of the octagon. Repeat the process on segments 3 and 7. Be sure the striped edges of the plywood are facing up. Draw cutting lines across the strips, using the edges of the octagon as a guide. Cut the strips flush with the edges of the octagon.

Attractive grain

For the most attractive grain match, cut both bowl blanks consecutively from the same board. Mark the top edge of each blank before cutting them apart to help keep the rings aligned.

5 **Attach the maple veneer.** Glue and clamp a piece of maple veneer to one face of the circle and let it dry. Trim the excess with a #2 blade, and then sand the veneer flush with the side of the circle. Use the same technique to glue a second piece of maple veneer to the other face, with the grain of both pieces of veneer running in the same direction.

EMBELLISH A BOWL WITH PLYWOOD: A STEP-BY-STEP GUIDE

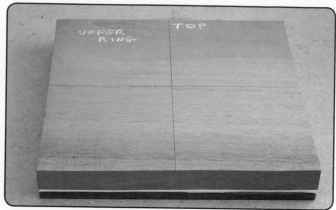

6 Complete the center ring. Reattach the pattern removed in Step 4 to the veneered accent-ring blank. Drill an entry hole where indicated on the pattern and cut the inner circle to create a plywood ring. The remainder of this blank is not used for this project.

7 Prepare the bowl blanks. Mark the two ¾" (19mm)-thick mahogany blanks to help you keep the grain aligned during glue-up. Choose one piece for the top ring and one for the bottom set of rings. Draw intersecting guidelines on both blanks. Then, glue and clamp the remaining piece of maple veneer and the square of ¼" (6mm)-thick mahogany to the underside of the blank for the top of the bowl. Let the glue dry.

8 Cut the outside of the top ring. Use repositionable adhesive to attach a bowl pattern to the upper face of the layered blank you assembled in Step 7. Use an awl to align the pattern with the guidelines. Tilt the left side of the saw table down to 28°, and cut clockwise along the outer line. *NOTE: You will invert this ring when you glue it to the accent ring (the thinnest layer is the bowl rim).*

Shop-made angle guide

On a scrap piece of wood, cut one edge at a 28° angle and the other edge at a 35° angle. Use the appropriate angle as a guide for the drill bit as you drill blade-entry holes for the rings.

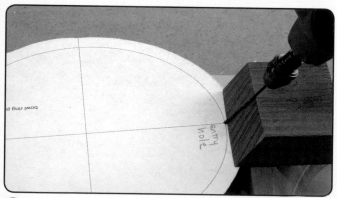

9 Drill a blade-entry hole. Mark the blade-entry hole on the pattern with an awl. Use a 35° angle guide (see Tip) to drill the hole, facing the center of the blank. The two different cutting angles give you extra wood to shape the opening of the bowl.

10 Cut the inside of the top ring. Tilt the left side of the saw table down to 35°. Insert the saw blade and cut clockwise along the inner circle. Mark the top of the ring and set it aside. The remainder of the blank is not needed for this project.

11 Cut the first bottom ring. Use spray adhesive to attach the second bowl pattern to the remaining piece of mahogany, aligning the pattern as in Step 8. Tilt the left side of the saw table down to 28°. Cut clockwise along the outer circle. Use a 28° angle guide to drill a blade-entry hole where indicated on the pattern, facing the center of the blank. Insert the saw blade and cut clockwise along the inner circle. Mark the top of the ring.

12 Mark the cutting line for the second ring. Place the ring on the remainder of the same blank, matching the top edges, and trace along the inside edge to form the cutting line for the second ring.

13 Cut the second bottom ring. Tilt the left side of the saw table down to 35°. Re-cut the outside of the blank to 35°, cutting clockwise. Do not cut into the top edge of the blank—use the top edge as the line to cut along. Use a 35° angle guide to drill a blade-entry hole on the line you drew in Step 12, facing the center of the blank. Insert the saw blade and cut clockwise around the inside of the ring with the table still angled to 35°. Mark the top of the ring.

14 Cut the base. Center the ring you cut in Step 13 on the remainder of the same blank, keeping the tops aligned. Trace the outside of the ring to form the cutting line for the base. Tilt the left side of the saw table down to 45° and cut clockwise along this line to form the base. Mark the top of the base and set it aside.

ASSEMBLING THE PROJECT

15 Glue the angled rings to the accent ring. Transfer the guidelines and top marks to the outsides of the rings, and then remove all of the marks from the gluing surfaces. Align and glue the top ring and first bottom ring to the plywood ring. The inner edges of the three rings will match, but the outside of the accent ring will protrude slightly to allow extra wood for shaping. Clamp the rings; I use a shop-made bowl press, but you can use clamps and scrap wood. Let the glue dry. *NOTE: In the photo, the bowl is upside down in the press.*

16 **Sand the inside of the rings.** Using a round inflatable sander and an 80-grit sleeve, sand the inside of the rings to remove any glue and irregularities. Then, use 150- and 220-grit sleeves to sand the assembly until smooth. Be careful when sanding near the lower edge of the bottom ring—you must leave enough wood to attach the next ring.

Sand instead of cut

If you have a sander with a tilting table, you can set the table to 45° and sand the base to the marked line. This is easier than cutting at a 45° angle.

17 **Attach the second bottom ring.** Glue the second bottom ring into place. Clamp, let dry, and sand the inside until smooth. Be sure the bottom edge of this ring is perfectly round to give the base an attractive appearance from the inside of the bowl.

18 **Attach the base.** Glue the base to the bottom ring, keeping the tops aligned. Clamp, wait 5 minutes for the glue to set, remove the clamps, and scrape off the excess glue. Re-clamp and let the bowl dry thoroughly.

19 **Sand the outside of the bowl.** Sand the outside of the bowl with a 2" (51mm) pad sander. Shape the accent ring and the sharp edge of the top ring to match the curvature of the bowl (see sidebar). Once you have completed the shaping, soften the inner edge of the opening with the round sander, and then sand with progressively finer grits until the bowl is smooth.

20 **Finish the bowl.** Apply mineral spirits to the bowl and use a white pencil to mark any glue spots that appear. Sand away these spots once the mineral spirits have dried. Apply a coat of spray shellac to seal the wood. Smooth the shellac with 0000 steel wool. Remove the dust with a vacuum and wipe the bowl before applying several coats of spray lacquer.

Sanding the outside of the bowl

1. (A) Start with the accent ring, sanding it from the center outward until it blends with the angled rings on either side. (B) Continue sanding from the accent ring outward until the sides are smooth and nicely shaped. (C) If the plywood ring resists smoothing, use a small detail sander to even it out.

2. Shape the sharp outer edge of the top ring to a smooth curve.

3. Sand the inside of the bowl opening to a soft edge, using the ring of maple veneer as a guide.

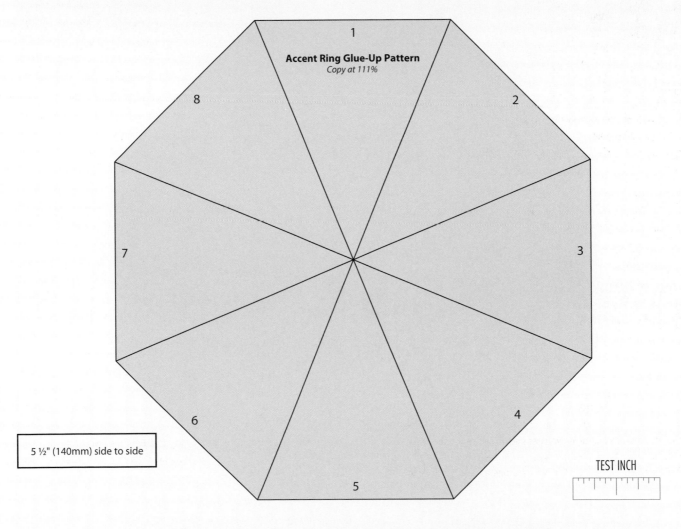

Accent Ring Glue-Up Pattern
Copy at 111%

1
2
3
4
5
6
7
8

5 ½" (140mm) side to side

TEST INCH

EMBELLISH A BOWL WITH PLYWOOD: A STEP-BY-STEP GUIDE

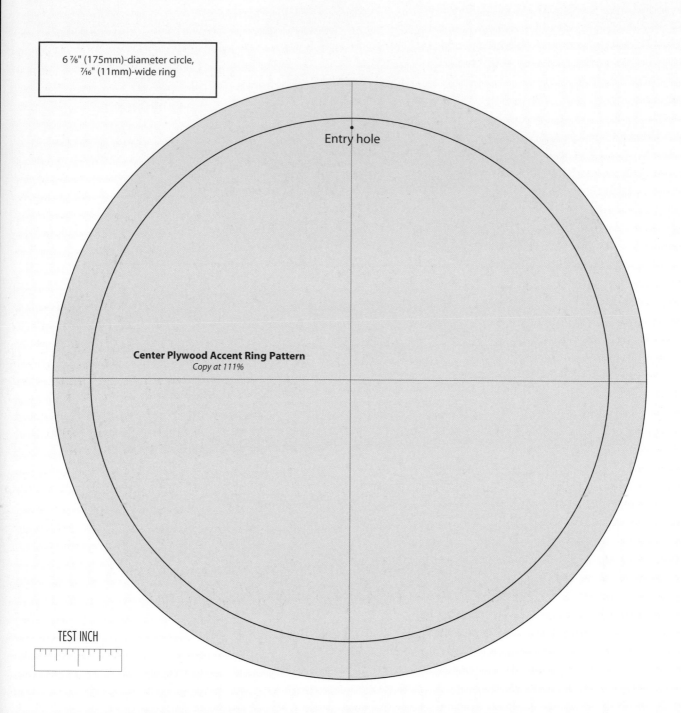

6 ⅞" (175mm)-diameter circle,
⅞₆" (11mm)-wide ring

Entry hole

Center Plywood Accent Ring Pattern
Copy at 111%

TEST INCH

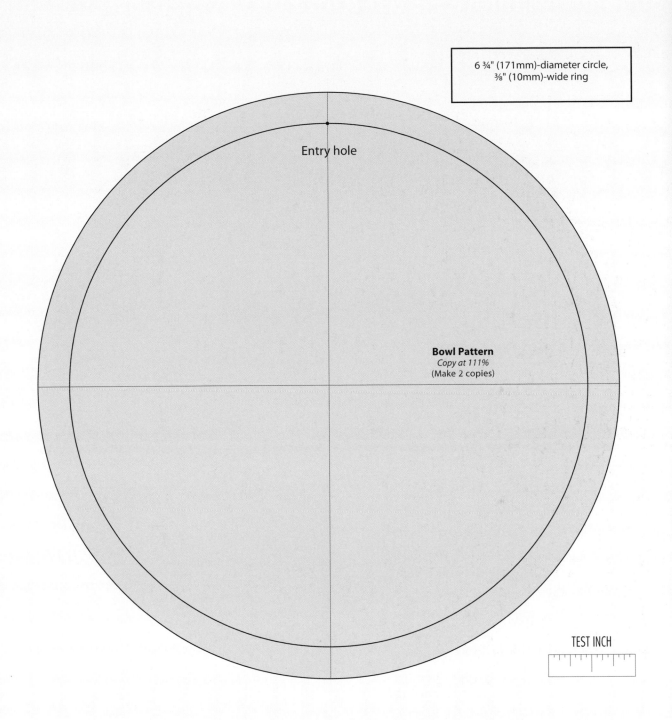

6 ¾" (171mm)-diameter circle,
⅜" (10mm)-wide ring

Entry hole

Bowl Pattern
Copy at 111%
(Make 2 copies)

TEST INCH

EMBELLISH A BOWL WITH PLYWOOD: A STEP-BY-STEP GUIDE

Spalted Sycamore Flared-Rim Bowl: A Step-by-Step Guide

Unique pieces of wood come with built-in dilemmas. On the one hand there's potential for great beauty, but on the other you have only one chance to get it right. I prefer simple shapes when working with intricately colored or highly figured wood, and reserve more elaborate profiles for wood with less character. For this colorful piece of spalted sycamore, I decided on a simple round bowl, but added a flared upper rim and contrasting brickwork pattern for interest. Finding a suitable wood to complement sycamore's warm brown and green tones took longer than anticipated, but I finally settled on teak. The results were worth the effort and served as a reminder that you'll seldom regret taking the time needed to do a job right.

Wood
- ⅞" x 9½" x 9½" (22mm x 241mm x 241mm) spalted sycamore (basic blank)
- ³⁄₁₆" x 9½" x 9½" (5mm x 241mm x 241mm) teak (laminate)
- (3) ³⁄₁₆" x ¹⁵⁄₁₆" x 9½" (5mm x 24mm x 241mm) teak (strips)
- (1) ⁵⁄₁₆" x 3½" x 3½" (8mm x 89mm x 89mm) teak (base)

Materials
- Wood glue, Weldbond preferred
- 150-grit sandpaper attached to a 12" (305mm) granite floor tile
- Repositionable adhesive
- Sandpaper for hand sanding
- Shellac sealer (one pound cut)
- Clear finish of choice

Tools
- Bowl press, or clamps and boards for gluing
- Shop-made angle guides: 17°, 25°, 30°
- Stationary sanders: Drum, SandFlee
- Inflatable sanders: large round, short drum, assorted grit sleeves
- 2" (51mm) pad sander, assorted discs
- Protractor
- Compass
- Drafting triangle
- Drill bits: #56 and #62
- #3 and #7 Pegas Super Skip blades

PREPARE THE BLANK

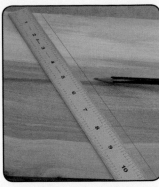

1 **Cut the sycamore blank in half.** Joint or sand the cut edges if not smooth and square. Glue the first teak strip between the sycamore halves, making sure that the strip and both pieces of sycamore are flush at the bottom. Clamp and let dry.

2 **Sand the top of the blank just until the teak strip is flush.** Draw a line down the center of the strip and locate its midpoint. Place a protractor on this line, zeroed at the midpoint. Draw a line at a 60° angle from that point and extend it to run fully across the blank.

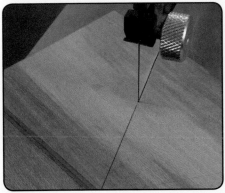

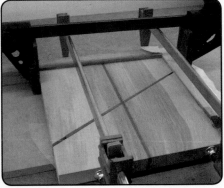

3 **Cut along the line drawn in Step 2.** Joint or sand the edges if not completely smooth. Mark the midpoint of the second teak strip. Glue in the strip, matching midpoints with the first strip and keeping the halves of the first strip aligned. If slippage occurs as you tighten the clamps, loosen them so you can slide the pieces back into place, then re-clamp, using minimal pressure. Let the glue dry completely.

4 **Sand the top of the blank as in Step 2.** Draw a line down the center of the second teak strip and mark where it intersects the center point of the first strip. From this point, use a protractor to draw a line at a 60° angle and extend it across the workpiece. Cut the line and smooth the edges as in Step 3.

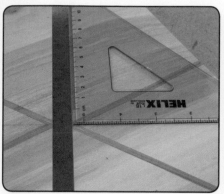

5 Align a drafting triangle with each cut edge of the workpiece and the "vee" formed by the first two strips. Draw a line along the lower edge of the drafting triangle. Mark the midpoint of the third strip. Align its center with the line you just drew and glue the strip into place. Note that all strips are not perfectly aligned; this will not affect the brick pattern.

6 Sand both faces of the blank. Finished thickness should be 13/16" (21mm) or slightly more. Place the blank, underside up, on your worktable. To locate the midpoint, re-draw the line across the "vees" as done in Step 5. Make an awl mark at the intersection of the line and the center of the third strip. Use a compass and this mark to draw a circle 9" in diameter. Draw a matching circle on the 3/16" (5mm) piece of teak, and cut the circles with the saw table level.

7 Apply glue generously to the upper (unmarked) face of the sycamore. Glue together the teak and sycamore circles, matching the edges and aligning the grain. Place in a press and clamp securely. To ensure a flat lamination, clamp the center in addition to the outer edges. When the glue has dried fully, measure the thickness of the laminated piece. It should be 1" (25mm) thick for best alignment. If thicker, sand away excess wood from the sycamore face, but make sure that the awl mark remains visible. (If it's over by less than 1/16" [16mm] and sanding is not feasible, you can use the blank as is.) Both faces should be smooth, level, and free of glue, and the piece should be evenly thick throughout.

MAKING THE BOWL

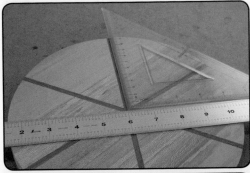

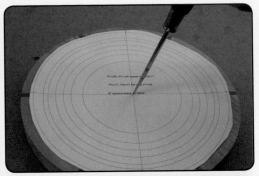

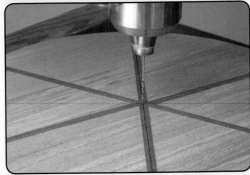

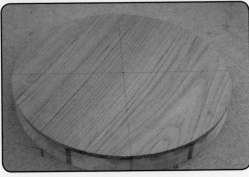

8 **Draw a registration line down the center of the third strip.** Draw a second line, perpendicular to the first, across the awl mark. Place the pattern on the blank to confirm correct positioning of your marks. The registration lines of the pattern and blank and the center point of the pattern and awl mark should all match. Remove the pattern. Transfer the center point to the teak side by drilling a through hole at the awl mark, using a #62 wire–size bit. Extend the registration lines down the sides of the blank and across the teak face. They should intersect at the drilled hole. This hole will be filled in Step 15.

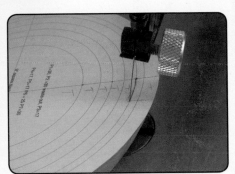

9 **Attach the pattern to the teak face with repositionable adhesive.** Use an awl to align the pattern with the drilled center hole and the registration lines. Tilt the left side of the saw table down to 30˚. Cut the first circle in a clockwise direction. Use an awl to mark the drill point on the *third* circle, where shown on the pattern. Drill a 17˚ blade entry hole at that mark, using a shop-made angle guide. Tilt the left side of the saw table down to 17˚. Insert the blade and cut in a clockwise direction to complete the first ring. Mark the top of this and every ring to help maintain the grain orientation during glue-up.

If your sanded blank is less than 1" (25mm) but at least ¹⁵⁄₁₆" (21mm) thick

Attach the pattern as in Step 9 and follow the instructions to cut the first ring, including the waste removal cut. Place that ring on the blank and compare its inside edge with the pattern cut line for the second ring. If they match, you can use the pattern. If not, keep the pattern attached and use your first ring to draw the cut line for the second ring. Cut that ring at 17˚. Use your second ring to draw the cut line for the third ring, the third for the fourth, and the fourth for the fifth, using the angles given in the instructions.

CHAPTER 3: Laminated Wood Bowls

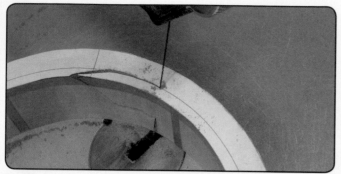

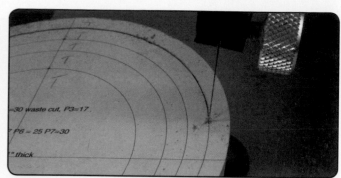

10 Tilt the left side of the saw table down to 30°. With the blade placed inside the ring, cut the second circle in a clockwise direction to remove excess wood and to establish the flare. Be careful not to cut into the bottom of the ring.

11 Drill and cut the second and third rings at 17° as in Step 9. Drill and cut the fourth ring at 25° and the fifth ring at 30°.

12 Stack the rings and base upside down, keeping the tops aligned. Rotate the second and fourth rings and the base slightly to the right so that their vertical strips are halfway between the strips of the adjacent rings. Rotate the stack carefully and adjust the components to obtain the best overall alignment. Draw several sets of pencil lines across the pieces to help with alignment during glue-up.

13 Stack the three smallest rings, keeping the alignment. Check carefully for spaces between them. Sand away uneven areas with a sheet of 150-grit sandpaper attached to a flat tile. Remove marks from the gluing surfaces, and "fuzzies" from the bottom edges. Glue the rings, clamp them in a press, and let the assembly dry.

14 Sand the inside of the rings until smooth. Use the round inflatable sander, starting with the coarse sleeve, then moving to the medium and fine sleeves. To preserve the gluing surface needed for Step 16, do not sand the upper edge of the top ring. Invert the rings to sand the lower edge into a smooth circle.

15 Remove pencil marks from the upper surface of the base. Fill the small center hole with a mixture of teak sawdust and glue. Sand the entire surface until smooth and level.

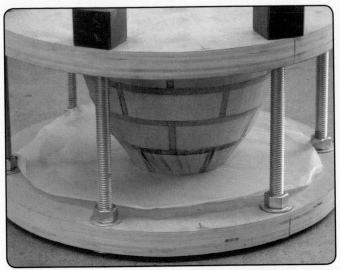

16 **Place the glued-up rings on the base.** Use the pencil marks for alignment and sand away any spaces that appear. Apply glue to the bottom ring, keeping the glue about ⅛" (3mm) from the inner edge to prevent squeeze-out. Place the ring assembly on the base and clamp the unit until the glue has set. Add the remaining two rings, matching registration marks and correcting any spaces. Clamp the bowl and let the glue dry fully.

17 **Sand and shape the two top rings.** Use the round inflatable sander and coarse sleeve, and follow the flare created in Step 10. Sand the inside top edge into a smooth circle, but do not flare it outward. This is done in Step 22. Smooth the joint between the second and third rings to create a continuous surface. Once the shaping is complete, switch to the medium and fine sleeves to smooth the surface.

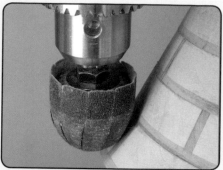

18 Smooth the joint on the outside of the bowl where the first and second rings meet. Use the round inflatable sander and coarse sleeve. This can be done with the bowl upright or inverted. Be careful not to create more than a slight indentation in the second ring as you smooth the joint. With bowl upright, gradually sand toward the teak rim as you deepen the curve. When the curve has been shaped, smooth the surface with the medium grit sleeve.

19 Invert the bowl. Use a compass centered at the midpoint of the base to draw a circle slightly smaller than the base. Use this circle as a reference point to keep your shaping symmetrical as you sand the lower portion of the bowl.

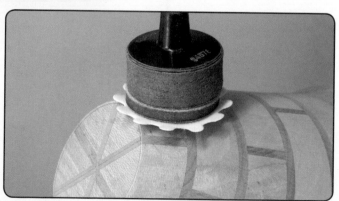

20 Shape the remainder of the bowl exterior. Start at the top of the second ring with the 2" (51mm) sander and 80-grit disc and blend the sanded flared area into the second ring. Work your way down to the base, removing blade and drill marks as you establish the shape. Work through the grits in small increments to 220, making sure to remove swirl marks as you move to higher grits. When the surface is smooth and free of bumps, sand the flared area with the round inflatable and fine sleeve.

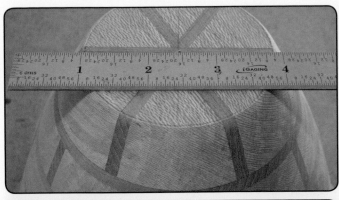

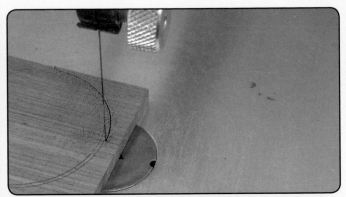

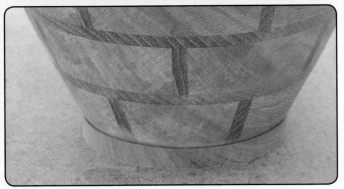

21 Invert the bowl and measure the base.

21 **Invert the bowl and measure the base.** To make the bottom piece, use a compass to draw a circle the size of the bowl base on the ⁵⁄₁₆" (8mm) piece of teak. Using the same center point, draw a second circle ⅛" (3mm) larger. With saw table level, cut to the outside of the outer circle and sand to that line with a vertical belt sander. Place the bowl on the bottom piece; it should protrude about ¹⁄₁₆" (2mm) all around. If you'd like a smaller reveal, reduce the size of the piece, using the inner circle as a reference as you sand. Make sure the bowl bottom and teak base are flat. Soften the upper and lower edges of the teak. Apply glue to the bowl bottom, but away from the edge to prevent squeeze-out. Clamp the piece briefly to establish a tight bond. Remove clamps, correct any slippage, and let the bowl dry without clamps.

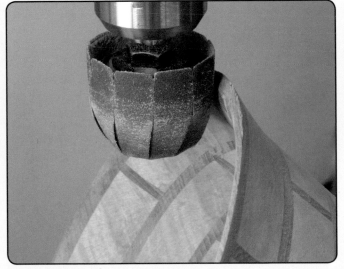

22 **Flare the top ring outward.** Start at the upper half of the top ring, using the round inflatable sander and medium grit sleeve. Sand around the ring, gradually flaring it outward as you move toward the teak rim. As you approach the rim, hold the sander almost parallel to the top face of the ring. You'll need to sand with the upper part of the sleeve to keep the open lower section from snagging on the edge. You can also use a small pneumatic drum to shape this area, angled to prevent gouges from its lower edge. Once the ring is shaped, use the fine sleeve to complete the sanding of the surface.

23 **Check the width of the teak area and mark any uneven places.** To even out and soften the edge, sand around the circumference using a pneumatic drum with a 220-grit sleeve. Hold the bowl firmly with both hands as you work around the rim for maximum control. Finish the rim with hand sanding.

24 **Apply a coat of mineral spirits to detect any glue spots.** Mark them with a white pencil. When the wood is dry, sand the glue spots and make a final check for irregularities. Then, apply a sealer coat of shellac. When it has dried, sand the bowl smooth with 320-grit sandpaper or a 320-grit sanding mop. Apply additional coats of shellac or finish of your choice.

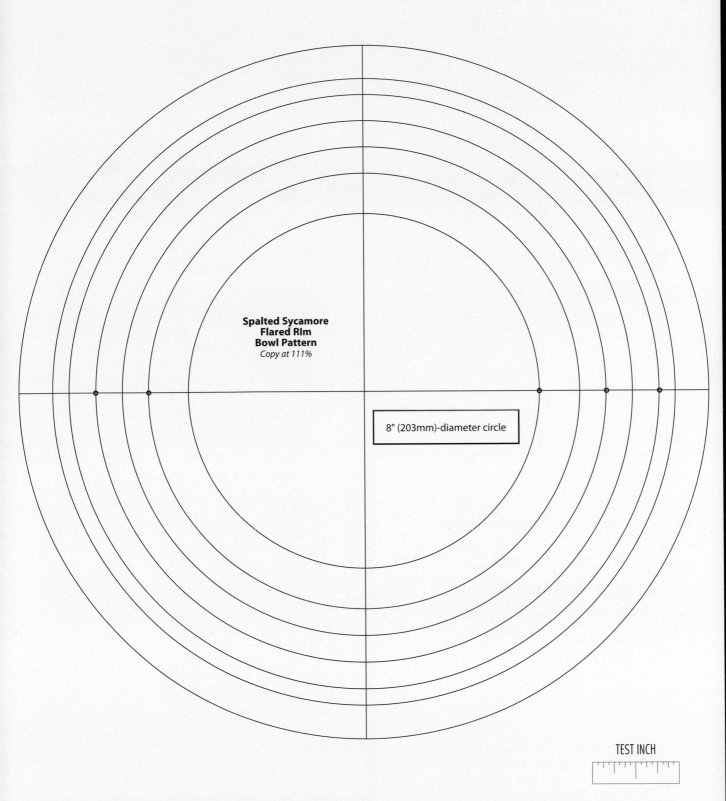

**Spalted Sycamore
Flared RIm
Bowl Pattern**
Copy at 111%

8" (203mm)-diameter circle

TEST INCH

SPALTED SYCAMORE FLARED-RIM BOWL: A STEP-BY-STEP GUIDE

Basket Duo: A Step-by-Step Guide

This economical project uses one simple glue-up to make two segmented blanks. By combining each with a matching piece of wood, you can make two complementary bowls with patterns that look like woven baskets. They can each be made with either straight or curved sides. Instructions are provided for both versions. Each is attractive and functional, and easy to cut and sand.

Wood
- ⅜" (10mm) x 8" (203mm) x 8" (203mm) walnut
- ⅜" (10mm) x 8" (203mm) x 8" (203mm) maple
- ⅞" (22mm) x 8" (203mm) x 8" (203mm) walnut (straight basket)
- ⅞" (22mm) x 5.5" (140mm) x 5.5" (140mm) walnut (straight basket base)
- ¾" (19mm) x 8" (203mm) x 8" (203mm) maple (curved basket)
- ¾" (19mm) x 5.5" (140mm) x 5.5" (140mm) maple (curved basket base)

Materials
- Double-sided tape
- Temporary bond adhesive
- Sandpaper for hand sanding
- 0000 steel wool
- Wood glue
- Spray shellac
- Clear spray gloss lacquer

Tools
- #5 polar blade, or #7 skip-tooth blade
- Drill bit size #54 (or smaller)
- Clamps or press for gluing rings
- Angle guides: 13° for straight-sided basket; 15°, 20°, 25° for curved-sided basket
- Awl
- 2" (51mm) or 3" (76mm) flexible pad sander and assorted grit discs
- Round, inflatable sander: coarse, medium, and fine sleeves
- Belt sander with tilting table

MAKING THE SEGMENTED BLANK

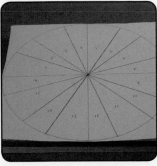
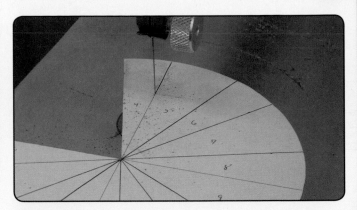

1 **Attach the pieces of ⅜" (10mm) walnut and maple to each other with thin strips of double-sided tape.** Clamp them together to secure the bond. Attach the segment pattern using temporary bond adhesive.

2 **Cut the circumference of the circle, then cut the segments.** Do not remove the pattern or separate the pairs.

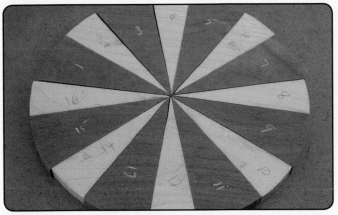

3 **Remove the pattern from each pair.** Write its number on each piece. Sand away "fuzzies" from the lower edges. Exchange the pieces to form two complete multi-colored blanks. One blank is used for each basket.

4 **Glue up one semicircle at a time.** Apply glue to one edge of the first segment. Rub that edge against the matching edge of the next segment until the glue drags. Continue adding segments in this manner, pressing the assembly against a straight edge or simple jig to ensure a flat edge when all eight segments are glued. Any segment tip that protrudes or interferes can be sanded down without affecting the finished basket.

5 **Sand or joint the straight edge of each semicircle.** The edges of each matching pair of semicircles should fit together without spaces. Join them by applying glue to one edge, then rub both edges together until they drag. Place the workpiece on a flat surface and let the glue dry. Sand both faces of the circle just until smooth and of even thickness. Final sanding will be done in Step 7. Use the circle with smaller walnut segments for the walnut basket, and the circle with the smaller maple segments for the maple basket.

CHAPTER 3: Laminated Wood Bowls

MAKING THE STRAIGHT-SIDED WALNUT BASKET

6 Draw a 7½" (191mm) circle on the ⅞" (22mm)-thick piece of walnut. Deepen the center mark with an awl. Cut the circle with saw table level.

7 Invert the walnut circle so that the awl mark is on the underside. Place the segmented blank on top and rotate it to match the grain of the walnut as closely as possible. Glue the pieces together, clamp, and let dry. Sand the laminated blank to a thickness of 1³⁄₁₆" (30mm). If it's a little thinner, but not less than 1⅛" (29mm), you can use the instructed cutting angle. If less than 1⅛" (29mm), use the instructions in the Appendix, page 186, to compute a new cutting angle.

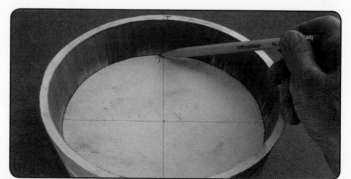

8 Attach the ring pattern to the walnut side, using an awl to match the centers. Using a shop-made angle guide, drill a 13° entry hole where indicated on the pattern. Tilt the saw table, left side down, to 13° and cut around the outer circle in a clockwise direction.

9 With the saw table at the same setting, insert the blade into the drilled entry hole. Cut clockwise around the inner circle to complete the first ring. Mark the top of the ring and the blank to help keep the alignment during glue-up. Do not remove the pattern from the pieces. The registration lines on the pattern, and top marks, will keep the rings oriented as you draw the cutting lines for the second and third rings.

10 Place the ring on the blank, with top marks aligned. Trace the inside of the first ring to draw the cutting line for the second ring. Drill a 13° entry hole opposite the one for the first ring. Insert the saw blade, cut the ring in a clockwise direction, and mark the top. Make the third ring in the same way. Remove all pattern pieces and transfer the top marks to the wood.

11 Stack the rings, matching top marks. Check for spaces between them and sand until they lie flat against each other. Glue the rings together, keeping the alignment, and clamp until dry.

Alternate design

To create an alternate design, rotate the second ring one segment to the left.

12 Sand the inside of the rings with a round inflatable sander. Use a coarse sleeve to smooth the sides and to remove blade and drill marks. Once that's completed, refine the surface with the medium grit sleeve. Finish with a fine sleeve, checking carefully for glue spots you may have missed. Be sure that the inside of the bottom ring is sanded into a smooth circle. You will not be able to sand this area once the bottom is attached.

13 Trace the outside of the rings on the remaining piece of ⅞" (22mm) walnut. Tilt the left side of the table down to 13°. Cut the circle in a clockwise direction to form the base. Place the rings on the base, aligning the grain. Check for and correct any spaces. Glue on the base and clamp the basket in a press. Remove the assembly after five minutes to clean up any squeeze-out, then replace it in the press and let the glue dry fully.

CHAPTER 3: Laminated Wood Bowls

Using the original base

If you have a drum sander, you can save wood and use the original base by sanding away the lamination. Since this will leave glue deposits on the sandpaper, use an old wrap for the job.

14 **Sand the outside of the basket.** Use a belt sander with the table tilted to 13°. I use a 120 or 150 grit belt to minimize scratch marks. Sand away visible scratch marks when you complete the sanding in Step 16.

15 **Create the bevel for the base in two steps.** First, tilt the sander table to 30° and sand halfway up the base. Then, set the table to 45° and sand halfway up the area that was beveled at 30°. This roughs out a gentle curve for the base.

16 **Complete the sanding of the exterior.** Use a 2" (51mm) or 3" (76mm) flexible pad sander to soften the bevel into a smooth curve. Sand the entire exterior progressively through the grits to 220.

17 **Use the round inflatable sander to soften the inner and outer edges of the top ring.** Finish sanding the basket by hand.

18 **Seal the wood with a coat of spray shellac.** Sand smooth with 320-grit sandpaper. Apply several coats of clear gloss lacquer, rubbing between coats with 0000 steel wool, as needed. Before adding a new coat, be sure to remove particles on the surface of the basket by vacuuming or by using a tack cloth.

Making the curved-sided maple basket

Follow these instructions to use the remaining segmented blank for the curved-sided maple basket

1. Start with Step 6, substituting the ¾" (19mm)-thick piece of maple for the ⅞" (22mm) piece of walnut. Glue up the blank as in Step 7, and sand to a total thickness of 1" (25mm).

2. Follow the instructions in Steps 8 and 9, but cut the first ring at 15°. Mark the top of the ring and remainder of the blank. Do not remove the pattern from either piece.

3. Draw the cutting line for the second ring as in Step 10. Drill a blade entry hole at 20°. Tilt the left side of the saw table down to 20°. Re-cut the outside of the blank to 20°, cutting in a clockwise direction and using the top edge as a guide. Insert the blade and cut the inside of the ring at 20°.

4. Place the second ring on the blank, aligning the top marks and registration lines. Trace the inner and outer edges. Drill a 25° blade entry hole on the inner circle. Tilt the left side of the saw table down to 25°. Cut the outer circle in a clockwise direction. Insert the blade into the entry hole and cut the inner circle, clockwise, at 25°.

5. Glue the rings as in Step 11. Sand the inside as in Step 12.

6. Follow the instructions in Step 13 for cutting and gluing on the base, using the remaining piece of ¾" (19mm)-thick maple and cutting the base at a 30° angle.

7. Sand the outside of the basket with a 2" (51mm) flexible pad sander. Start with a coarse grit and sand progressively through the grits to 220-grit.

8. Follow Steps 17 and 18 to complete the basket.

B

C

D

A

CHAPTER 3: Laminated Wood Bowls

Basket Duo Pattern
Copy at 111%

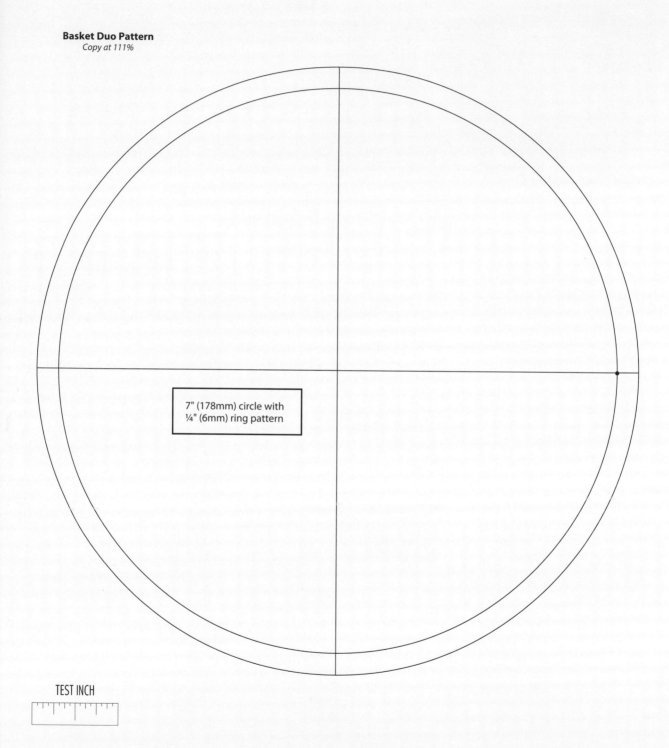

7" (178mm) circle with
¼" (6mm) ring pattern

TEST INCH

Basket Duo Pattern
Copy at 111%

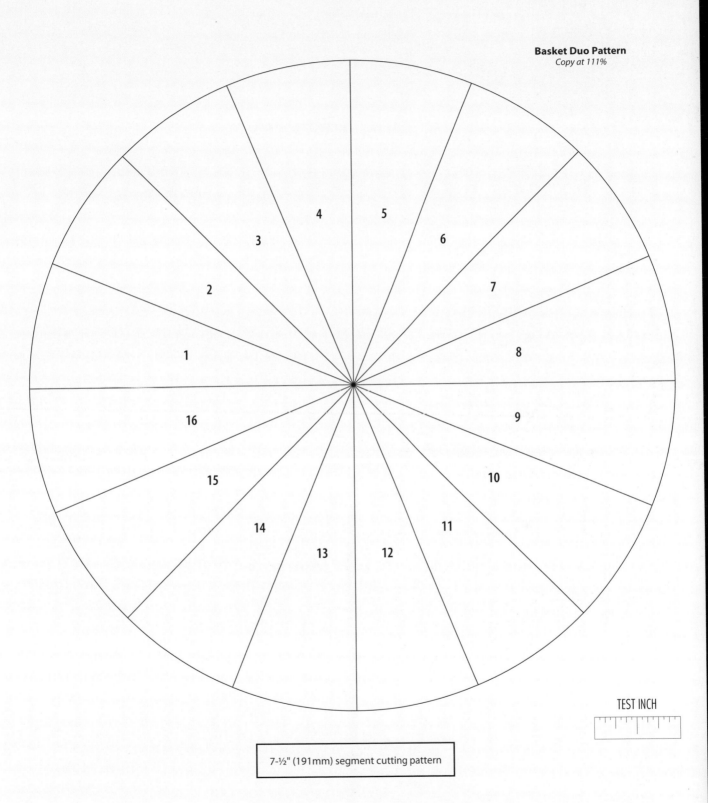

4

5

3

6

2

7

1

8

16

9

15

10

14

11

13

12

TEST INCH

7-½" (191mm) segment cutting pattern

BASKET DUO: A STEP-BY-STEP GUIDE

Basket Weave Bowl

The plans for this bowl came about quite by accident. I was trying to make a colorful bowl with vertical stripes and inadvertently rotated one of the rings. Almost by magic, a basket weave pattern appeared. The effect was so compelling that I abandoned my original project and focused on ways to make the bowl look as much like a basket as possible. Because the laminated blank was fairly thick, I was able to use a smaller cutting angle to reduce the flare of the sides. Cutting four rings, rather than three, added to the bucket-like appearance, and a separate thin base yielded better proportions than a thick one.

Wood

BOWL:
- (1) 7½" x 7½" x ¾" (191mm x 191mm x 19mm) cedar
- (1) 7½" x 7½" x ¼" (191mm x 191mm x 6mm) padauk

VERTICAL STRIPS:
- (3) 7½" x 1" x ¼" (191mm x 25mm x 6mm) poplar

BASE:
- (1) 4½" x 4½" x ¼" (114mm x 114mm x 6mm) padauk

Materials
- Packing tape (optional)
- Glue
- Sanding discs for flexible pad sander, assorted grits 60 to 400
- Sandpaper for inflatable ball sander, assorted grits 60 to 320 (optional)
- Sandpaper for hand sanding, assorted grits 220 to 400
- 0000 steel wool or 320-grit sanding sponge
- Spray shellac or Danish oil

Tools
- Scroll saw blade, size #9
- Drill bit size #54 or 1/16" (2mm)
- Ruler
- Protractor
- Compass
- Bowl press or clamps
- Clamps for lamination
- 2" (51mm) flexible pad sander
- Inflatable ball sander and pump (optional)

1 **Glue the first strip.** Glue the 7½" (191mm) piece of padauk to the cedar, keeping the grains running in the same direction. Clamp and let dry. Cut the blank in half along the grain. Smooth the cut edges. Glue the first poplar strip between the cut edges. Clamp and let dry.

2 **Mark the center of the first strip.** Draw a line through the center of the poplar strip. Mark the center of the blank.

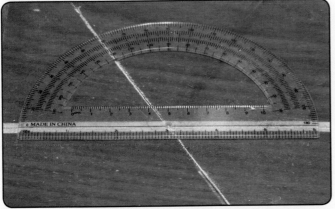

3 **Draw the cutting line for the second strip.** Center the protractor on the line drawn in Step 2. Use the protractor to mark a 60° angle. Draw a line through the blank at that angle.

4 **Glue in the second strip.** Cut the blank on the line drawn in Step 3. Smooth the cut edges. Glue the second poplar strip between the cut edges. Clamp and let dry. Draw a line through the center of the second strip. Mark a 60° angle in the same manner as the first strip. Cut on the line and smooth the edges.

5 **Glue in the third strip.** Glue in the third poplar strip. Clamp and let dry. Orient the blank so that the third strip is vertical and the V shapes formed by the first two pieces of poplar are directly opposite each other. Draw a line through the middle of the third strip. At the center point of the third strip, draw a line that is perpendicular to the line you just drew. This line should run through the center of the V shapes. These are your guidelines.

Note: Your blank is now divided into six segments. Don't be concerned about the apparent lack of alignment in the middle. The center piece left after the rings have been cut will be replaced by a solid piece of padauk to form the bottom of the bowl.

CHAPTER 3: Laminated Wood Bowls

MAKING THE BOWL

1. Using the center point on the poplar, draw a 7" (178mm)-diameter circle with a compass.

2. Draw a second circle ⅜" (10mm) inside the first circle.

3. Tilt scroll saw table 22°, left side down.

4. Cut the bowl outline in a clockwise direction.

5. Mark the top of the outer rim.

6. Drill a 22° entry hole and cut out the first ring.

7. Check ring alignment and adjust the angle if needed. Mark the top.

8. Use the inside of each ring to mark the outline for the next ring.

9. Cut three additional rings. Mark the top of each. The remaining piece of the blank will not be used.

10. Stack the rings. To create the basket weave effect, rotate each ring so the poplar strips are between the poplar strips of the ring below. Rings one and three should be aligned with each other, as should rings two and four.

11. Check for spaces.

12. Glue the rings, clamp them, and let dry.

13. Sand the inside of the bowl smooth.

14. Place the bowl on the remaining ¼" (6mm) piece of padauk and mark the outline of the bottom ring.

15. Tilt the saw table 22°, left side down, and cut the piece of padauk along the outline, cutting clockwise.

16. Glue this piece to the bottom of the rings to form the base. Clamp the bowl and let dry.

17. Sand the outside of the bowl and the upper edge.

18. Apply finish of choice.

10 **Setting the rings.** Align each ring so the poplar strips are located between the poplar strips of the ring below.

Alternate version

To make the alternate version of this bowl, you will need to make the following changes to the materials and instructions:

• Primary wood is ¾" (19mm) mahogany, not ¾" (19mm) cedar

Working with padauk

I decided to use cedar as the primary wood, with padauk and poplar laminations. I loved the color combination, but found that the sanding dust from the padauk tended to settle into the soft surface of the cedar. I solved that problem by vacuuming frequently as I sanded, but discovered during finishing that if I wet the padauk too heavily with shellac, the orange color bled into the cedar. After sanding off the discoloration, I used very light coats and had no further problems. If you want to avoid this situation, replace the cedar with a denser or darker wood.

Plaid Bowl

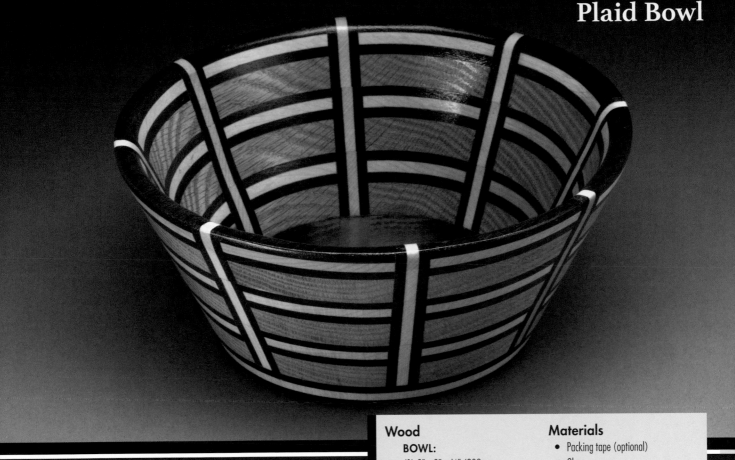

Fabrics are a good source of ideas for laminations. I was able to create a plaid effect by combining two lamination techniques: stacking and gluing layers of wood, and gluing in strips. The lamination, which is done in stages, is not difficult, but does require more wood than usual. However, I think the uniqueness of the bowl justifies the extra cost. I chose oak as the base wood because it contrasts well with purpleheart and maple. These woods are also of similar hardness, which facilitates sanding and finishing.

Wood

BOWL:
- (1) 8" x 8" x ½" (203mm x 203mm x 13mm) oak
- (1) 8" x 8" x 1/8" (203mm x 203mm x 3mm) maple
- (2) 8" x 8" x 1/8" (203mm x 203mm x 3mm) purpleheart

STRIPS:
- (8) 8" x 1" x 1/8" (203mm x 25mm x 3mm) purpleheart
- (4) 8" x 1" x 1/8" (203mm x 25mm x 3mm) maple
- **Note:** The strips are cut slightly wide to allow for sanding the striped faces.

BASE:
- (2) 6" x 6" x 1/8" (152mm x 152mm x 3mm) purpleheart
- (1) 6" x 6" x 1/8" (152mm x 152mm x 3mm) maple

Materials
- Packing tape (optional)
- Glue
- Sanding discs for flexible pad sander, assorted grits 60 to 400
- Sandpaper for inflatable ball sander, assorted grits 60 to 320 (optional)
- Sandpaper for hand sanding, assorted grits 220 to 400
- 0000 steel wool or 320-grit sanding sponge
- Spray shellac or Danish oil

Tools
- Scroll saw blade, size #9
- Drill bit size #54 or 1/16" (2mm)
- Ruler
- Compass
- Bowl press or clamps
- Clamps for lamination
- 2" (51mm) flexible pad sander
- Inflatable ball sander and pump (optional)

LAMINATION GUIDE

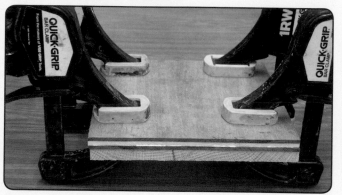

1 Glue the blank. Glue the 8" x 8" (203mm x 203mm) pieces of wood in the following order: oak, purpleheart, maple, purpleheart. Be sure all grain runs in the same direction. Clamp and let dry.

2 Glue the strips. Glue the 8" x 1" x ⅛" (203mm x 25mm x 3mm) pieces of stock to make four separate strips. Each strip is glued in the following order: purpleheart, maple, purpleheart. Clamp and let dry. Sand the striped faces smooth.

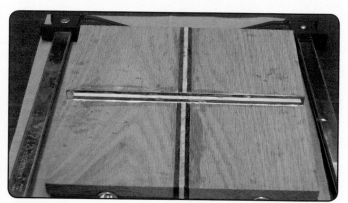

3 Insert the first strip. Cut the 8" x 8" (203mm x 203mm) blank into two pieces, cutting with the grain. Each piece will measure 8" x 4" (203mm x 102mm). Sand the cut edges smooth. Glue one of the laminated strips, striped face up, between the two pieces. Check the edges of the blank to be sure the two halves are aligned. Clamp and let dry.

4 Insert the second strip. Cut the newly glued-up blank in half, this time cutting across the grain. Glue a second laminated strip between the halves. Check the alignment. Clamp and let dry.

5 Insert the third strip. Draw diagonal lines from corner to corner, passing through the center point. Cut along one of the diagonal lines. Sand the cut faces smooth. Glue the third laminated strip between the halves. Clamp and let dry.

6 Insert the fourth strip. Cut along the other diagonal line and repeat Step 5. Sand the top and bottom surfaces smooth with a drum or hand sander. Be sure the blank is flat and even. Because multiple layers of wood have been sandwiched, check the final thickness and adjust the cutting angle if needed.

MAKING THE BOWL

1. With the purple side up, locate the center of the bowl blank. Please note all rings are cut on this side.

2. Draw a 7" (178mm)-diameter circle with a compass.

3. Draw a second circle ⅜" (10mm) inside the first circle.

4. Tilt the scroll saw table 24°, left side down.

5. Cut the outer circle in a clockwise direction.

6. Mark the top of the outer rim.

7. Drill a 24° entry hole and complete the first ring.

8. Check ring alignment and adjust the angle if needed. Mark the top.

9. Use the first ring to mark the outline for the second ring.

10. Cut the second ring. Mark and cut the third ring.

11. Stack the rings, checking for alignment and spaces.

12. Glue the rings, clamp them, and let dry.

13. Sand the inside of the bowl smooth.

14. Choose type of base, gluing pieces together if using the thin laminated base. (See sidebar, Choosing a base, right.)

15. Place the bowl on the base and mark the outline, if using the thin laminated base or the ¼" (6mm)-thick purpleheart base.

16. Cut the base at 24° if using the thin laminated base or the ¼" (6mm)-thick purpleheart base, saw table tilted left side down, cutting clockwise.

17. Glue on the base. Clamp and let dry.

18. Sand the outside of the bowl and upper edge.

19. Apply finish of choice.

Choosing a base

Different effects can be obtained by varying the type of base used for the bowl.

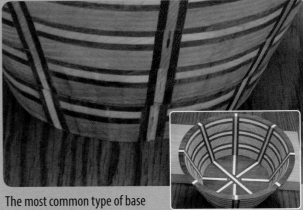

The most common type of base is formed by using the remainder of the bowl blank after cutting the rings. This choice continues the lamination pattern on both outside and inside the bowl.

A second choice is to laminate wood to produce a thinner matching base with a solid color face. To make this base, glue up the 6" (152mm) squares of ⅛" (3mm) purpleheart and maple, sandwiching the maple between the purpleheart.

A third choice is to use ¼" (6mm)-thick purpleheart.

CHAPTER 3: Laminated Wood Bowls

Gingham Bowl

Gingham-patterned fabric was the inspiration for this bowl. The laminated inserts are quick and easy to do, and when glued into the bowl blank and cut at an angle, they form patterns that look remarkably like gingham checks. I chose a light background to highlight the laminations, but a darker wood would also work well.

Wood

BOWL:
- (1) 8" x 8" x ¾" (203mm x 203mm x 19mm) maple

A STRIPS:
- (2) 8" x 1½" x ¼" (203mm x 38mm x 6mm) purpleheart
- (1) 8" x 1½" x ¼" (203mm x 38mm x 6mm) cherry

B STRIPS:
- (2) 8" x ¾" x ¼" (203mm x 19mm x 6mm) cherry
- (1) 8" x ¾" x ¼" (203mm x 19mm x 6mm) oak

Materials
- Packing tape (optional)
- Glue

- Sanding discs for flexible pad sander, assorted grits 60 to 400
- Sandpaper for inflatable ball sander, assorted grits 60 to 320 (optional)
- Sandpaper for hand sanding, assorted grits 220 to 400
- 0000 steel wool or 320-grit sanding sponge
- Spray shellac or Danish oil

Tools
- Scroll saw blade, size #9
- Drill bit size #54 or ¹⁄₁₆" (2mm)
- Ruler
- Compass
- Bowl press or clamps
- Clamps for lamination
- 2" (51mm) flexible pad sander
- Inflatable ball sander and pump (optional)

LAMINATION GUIDE

1 Glue up the strips. Glue up the pieces for strips A and B so that the contrasting piece is sandwiched between the other two. Clamp and let dry. Sand the striped faces smooth.

2 Complete the strips. Cut four ¼" (6mm) slices from the A strips, cutting parallel to the striped face. Cut two ¼" (6mm) slices from the B strips, cutting parallel to the striped face. Sandwich one B strip between two A strips. Glue and clamp them. Repeat with the remaining set of strips.

3 Glue in the strips. Cut the maple bowl blank in half along the grain. Sand the cut edges smooth. Insert one strip between the halves. Glue, clamp, and let dry. Cut the bowl blank in half across the grain. Sand the cut edges smooth. Insert the remaining strip between the halves, glue, clamp and let dry. Sand the laminated blank smooth.

Alternate version

To make the alternate version of this bowl, you will need to make the following changes to the materials and instructions:

- Outer circle is 6¾" (171mm), not 7" (178mm)
- Primary wood is ¾" (19mm) lacewood, not ¾" (19mm) maple
- Strip A is made of ¼" (6mm) maple and ¼" (6mm) oak, not ¼" (6mm) purpleheart and ¼" (6mm) cherry
- Strip B is made of ¼" (6mm) oak and ¼" (6mm) purpleheart, not ¼" (6mm) cherry and ¼" (6mm) oak
- Ring width is ½" (13mm) instead of ⅜" (10mm)
- Cutting angle is 34° instead of 28°
- 4 rings are cut, not 3
- Base is inverted and sanded to about ¼" (6mm)

MAKING THE BOWL

1. Locate the center of the bowl blank.
2. Draw a 7" (178mm)-diameter circle with a compass.
3. Draw a second circle ⅜" (10mm) inside the first circle.
4. Tilt the scroll saw table 28°, left side down.
5. Cut the bowl outline in a clockwise direction.
6. Mark the top of the outer rim.
7. Drill an entry hole at a 28° angle and cut out the first ring.
8. Mark the top of each ring.
9. Use the inside of each ring to mark the outline for the next ring.
10. Cut two additional rings, marking the top of each.
11. Stack the rings so that the laminated pieces are staggered.
12. Check for spaces between the rings.
13. Glue the rings, clamp them, and let dry.
14. Sand the inside of the bowl smooth.
15. Glue on the base, making sure to stagger the lamination. Clamp and let dry.
16. Sand the outside and upper edge of the bowl.
17. Apply finish of choice.

These projects incorporate multiple cutting angles, which allow for more drastic changes in the shapes of the bowls.

Multiple-Angle Bowls

The bowls in previous chapters are made from blanks, either plain or laminated, that are cut into concentric rings. What differentiates the bowls in this chapter from many that appear earlier is that for each bowl the cutting angle is increased as the rings become smaller. Depending on the magnitude of the change, the effect on the shape of the sides, bottoms, and top rings can be subtle or dramatic. This approach vastly increases the options available for bowls made with the scroll saw.

Crisscross Bowl: A Step-by-Step Guide

Combining dark teak and light maple creates a striking yet easy-to-make bowl. The bowl blank is laminated in several steps to produce a crisscross look. To achieve the effect of a separate base, the lower edge of the glued-up rings and upper edge of the base are contoured separately before being glued together. This unusual effect was created by accident when I rounded the lower edge of the glued-up rings by mistake and needed to figure out some way to save the bowl.

Wood
- (1) 9" x 8" x ¾" (229mm x 203mm x 19mm) teak
- (2) 12" x 1¼" x ¾" (305mm x 32mm x 19mm) maple

Materials
- Packing tape (optional)
- Glue
- Repositionable adhesive
- Sanding discs for flexible pad sander, assorted grits 60 to 400
- Sandpaper for inflatable ball sander, assorted grits 60 to 320 (optional)
- Sandpaper for hand sanding, assorted grits 220 to 400
- 0000 steel wool or 320-grit sanding sponge
- Spray shellac or Danish oil

Tools
- Scroll saw blade, size #9
- Drill bit size #54 or 1/16" (2mm)
- Awl
- Ruler
- Bowl press or clamps
- Clamps for lamination
- 2" (51mm) flexible pad sander
- Inflatable ball sander and pump (optional)

LAMINATION GUIDE

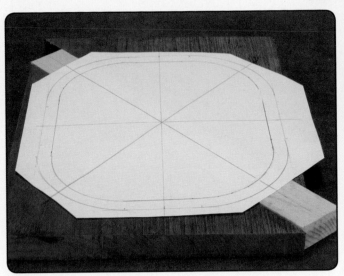

1 **Insert the first maple strip.** Make two copies of the pattern (page 87): one for the lamination and the other for cutting the rings. Cut the teak diagonally from point to point. Insert one of the maple strips, keeping the grain of the teak aligned. Glue, clamp, and let dry.

2 **Make the second cut.** Draw a line down the center of the maple strip. Align the pattern with that line and attach with repositionable adhesive. Use the pattern to mark the ends of the second diagonal. Draw the second diagonal on the wood and cut along that line.

3 **Complete the lamination.** Insert the second piece of maple between the cut edges of the teak, keeping the grain of the teak aligned. Glue, clamp, and let dry. Trim off the protruding edges, if desired, to make blank easier to handle.

Gluing on the diagonal

Gluing up wood cut on the diagonal can be tricky. Glue that sets up quickly with a good "grab," such as Weldbond, makes the process easier. If you rub the glued pieces together to force out air bubbles and let them set up for a minute or two, they will be less likely to slide when you apply the clamp. If you still get slippage, remove the clamp, slide the pieces carefully back into position without breaking the seal, and let them dry without clamping. If the pieces mated properly, the clamping that was done should be sufficient to obtain a good join.

CHAPTER 4: Multiple-Angle Bowls

CRISSCROSS BOWL: A STEP-BY-STEP GUIDE

MAKING THE BOWL

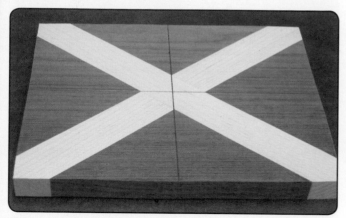

1 **Drawing the guidelines.** Using the crossed maple pieces as a guide, draw intersecting guidelines on the bowl blank.

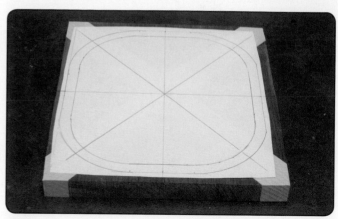

2 **Gluing the pattern.** Apply repositionable adhesive to the pattern. Push the point of an awl through the center of the pattern and place the point on the center of the bowl blank. Align the pattern with the guidelines drawn on the wood.

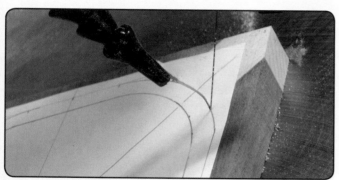

3 **Cutting the outline.** Tilt saw table to 30°, left side down. Cut clockwise along the outer line.

4 **Drilling the entry hole for the first ring.** Using a tilting drill press or 30° angle guide, drill an entry hole on the inner circle at 30°, angled toward the center of the blank.

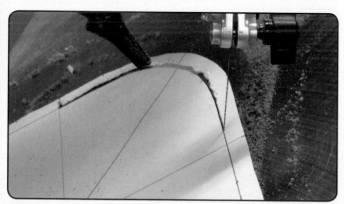

5 **Completing the first ring.** Insert the blade through the entry hole and cut clockwise along the line to complete the first ring.

6 **Marking the first ring.** Place the ring on the blank, mark the top, and transfer the guidelines from the blank. The blank may be slightly larger than the ring because of the steeper cutting angle. This will be sanded smooth when you shape the outside of the bowl.

7 **Outlining the second ring.** Keeping the first ring in place on the blank, trace the inside of the first ring. This is the cutting line for the second ring.

8 **Drilling the entry hole for the second ring.** Drill a 28° entry hole on the second ring, using an angle guide or a tilting drill press. This change in angle gives a gentle flare to the top ring.

9 **Cutting the second ring.** Tilt the scroll saw table to 28°, left side down. Insert the blade through the entry hole and cut clockwise on the marked line.

10 **Marking the second ring and tracing outline for third ring.** Place the second ring on the blank, mark the top, and transfer the guidelines. Trace the inside of the second ring to form the outline for the third ring.

11 **Cutting the third ring.** Drill a 28° entry hole and cut the third ring at a 28° angle. The remaining piece will become the base.

12 **Cutting the base.** Tilt the saw table 35°, left side down. Using the top edge of the base as a guide, cut around the base clockwise. Do not cut into the top of the base. The purpose of this cut is to increase the angle of the base.

CRISSCROSS BOWL: A STEP-BY-STEP GUIDE

13 **Preparing the rings.** Stack the three rings and check for spaces. Sand if necessary. Transfer all marks to the outer and inner edges and erase all marks from the top surface of the lower rings.

14 **Gluing the rings.** Glue the three rings together, keeping the maple stripes aligned. Clamp the rings and let them dry.

15 **Sanding the rings.** Sand the inner and outer faces of the rings until they are smooth, using the inflatable ball and flexible pad sanders.

16 **Shaping the top ring.** Accentuate the flare in the top ring using the flexible pad sander.

17 **Shaping the bottom ring.** Sand the lower edge into a curved shape.

18 **Shaping the base.** Using the flexible pad sander, contour the upper edge of the base into a curved shape to match the lower edge of the rings. Sand the entire base smooth.

19 Gluing on the base. Glue the base to the ring assembly. Clamp the bowl and let dry.

20 Finishing the bowl. Apply mineral spirits to the bowl to reveal any glue spots. Mark them with a white pencil or chalk. When the bowl is dry, sand off the glue spots. Apply the first coat of shellac and let dry. Smooth the surface with a 320-grit sanding sponge or 0000 steel wool. Vacuum, remove any remaining particles with a damp cloth or paper towel, and recoat. Repeat until the desired finish is obtained.

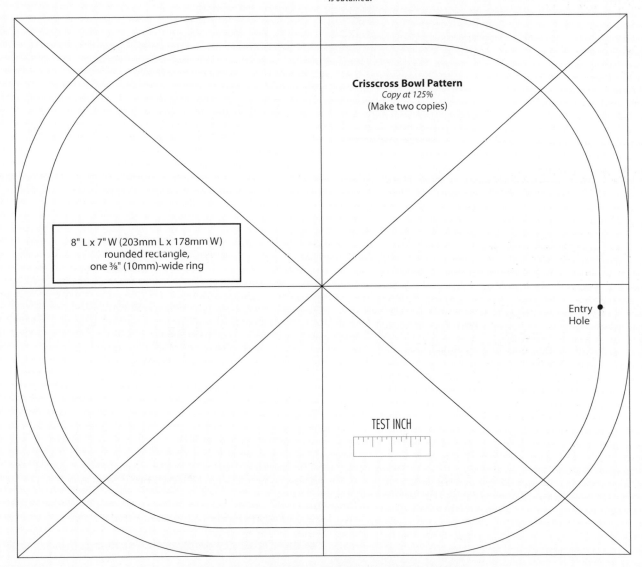

Crisscross Bowl Pattern
Copy at 125%
(Make two copies)

8" L x 7" W (203mm L x 178mm W)
rounded rectangle,
one ⅜" (10mm)-wide ring

Entry
Hole

TEST INCH

CRISSCROSS BOWL: A STEP-BY-STEP GUIDE

Scrolled Yarn Bowl: A Step-by-Step Guide

I learned to knit when I was eight, but saw my first yarn bowl only recently at a local crafts fair. Although the one I saw was made of ceramic, I saw its potential as a wooden scrolled bowl. I worked up some prototypes and took them to my local knitting store, the Yarn & Craft Box in Pawling, N.Y., for a trial run and critique.

Using feedback from my testers, I designed a rectangular "Asian style" yarn bowl. The generous interior and relatively flat sides make cutting the slot fairly simple. If you can't reach all parts of the slot pattern with a flat blade, use a small spiral to complete the job, and then sand the opening to a silky smoothness.

Whether made as shown or without the cutouts and the base, this versatile bowl is a fun project that's sure to please.

Wood

- Cherry ¾" (19mm) thick: bowl, 7½" x 9½" (191mm x 241mm)
- Cherry, ¾" (19mm) thick: base, 4½" x 6" (114mm x 152mm)
- Purpleheart, ⅛" (3mm) thick: base, 2 each 4" x 6" (102mm x 152mm)

Materials

- Repositionable adhesive
- Wood glue
- Sandpaper
- Small weights, such as BBs, lead sinkers, or lead shot
- Clear packaging tape
- Epoxy or caulk
- Shellac
- Beeswax and mineral oil finish

Tools

- Scroll saw blades: #9, #5, #2 skip or reverse-tooth; #2⁄0 spiral
- Drill with bits: #54 or 1⁄16" (2mm), ⅜" (10mm) brad-point
- Awl
- Rotary tool with bits: carbide burrs, sanding drums
- Round inflatable sander and sleeves
- 2" flexible pad sander and discs
- Random orbital sander (optional)
- Bowl press or clamps and boards
- Shop-made angle guides: 23°, 28°, 35°

CUTTING THE RINGS

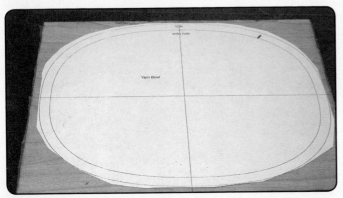

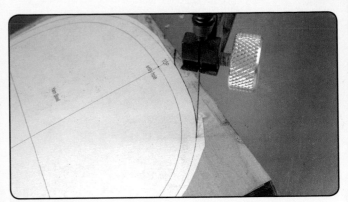

1 Prepare to cut. Draw intersecting guidelines down the center of the bowl blank. For stability, the long sides of the bowl must follow the grain direction. Mark the top edge of the blank with a pencil and cover the blank with packaging tape to prevent burning. Align the guidelines on the blank and pattern, and attach the pattern to the wood with repositionable adhesive.

2 Cut the perimeter of the first ring. Tilt the left side of the saw table down 23° and cut the perimeter of the first ring in a clockwise direction.

3 Cut the center of the first ring. Mark the location of the blade-entry hole with an awl and use a guide to drill the hole at a 23° angle facing the center of the blank. Insert the blade and cut in a clockwise direction around the inside of the ring. Mark the top edges of both the completed ring and the remainder of the blank.

4 Draw the second ring. Place the first ring on the blank, aligning the top edges and the guide lines. Trace the inside of the ring onto the blank to mark the cutting line for the second ring.

5 Cut the second ring. Mark a blade-entry hole with an awl opposite to the first blade-entry hole (to avoid back-to-back drill marks). Drill a blade-entry hole at a 23° angle on the mark, facing the center of the blank. Insert the blade and cut clockwise to complete the second ring. Mark the top of the ring.

CHAPTER 4: Multiple-Angle Bowls

6 **Cut the third ring.** Trace the inside of the second ring onto the blank with the tops aligned. Then, tilt the left side of the saw table to 28°. Use the top edge of the blank as a guide as you cut clockwise around the perimeter to create a steeper angle on the outside of the ring. Drill a blade-entry hole at 28°, facing the center of the blank. Insert the blade and cut clockwise with the table at the same angle. Mark the top of the ring.

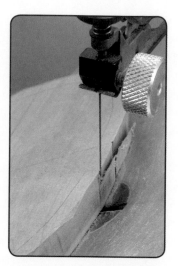

7 **Cut the fourth ring.** Place the third ring on the blank, and trace the inner and outer edges to form the cutting lines for the fourth ring. Tilt the left side of the saw table down to 35° and cut the perimeter clockwise. Drill the blade-entry hole at a 35° angle, keep the table angle the same, and cut the inside of the ring clockwise. Mark the top of the ring.

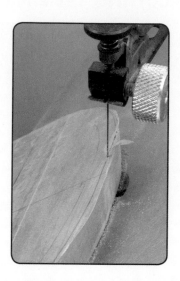

8 **Cut the bottom piece.** Place the fourth ring on the blank, aligning the tops and guidelines. Trace the outside of the ring to form the cutting line for the bottom piece. With the table tilted at a 35° angle, cut clockwise around the line.

ASSEMBLING THE BOWL

9 **Dry-assemble the rings.** Check for spaces between them. Remove the pencil marks from the gluing surfaces, and transfer the top marks to the sides of the rings. Do not remove the center marks on the top ring. Sand the rings as needed until they lie flat and no light can be seen between the rings when stacked. I use a sheet of sandpaper attached to a flat surface.

10 **Glue the rings together.** I use a bowl press (plans for shop-made versions can be found online), but you can use clamps and boards. Keep the top marks of each ring aligned as you clamp them tight. Allow the glue to dry. Do not glue on the bottom or base at this time.

11 **Sand the inside of the bowl.** Use a round inflatable sander. Keep sanding, working from coarse to finer grits, until the sides are smooth and the bottom has a regular shape that follows the contours of the bowl.

12 **Attach the bottom.** Apply glue to the underside of the bottom ring, and put the bowl bottom in position. Clamp it and allow the glue to set for five minutes. Remove the clamps and scrape off any glue squeeze-out on the surface of the bottom piece. Replace the clamps and allow the glue to dry.

13 **Sand the outside of the bowl.** Use a flexible pad sander in a drill press. Start with coarse grit to remove the excess wood and glue, and to establish the shape. Work up through the grits to smooth the surface and remove the scratches from previous grits. You can also use a small random orbital sander to obtain a smooth surface on the outer face of the bowl.

MAKING THE WEIGHTED BASE

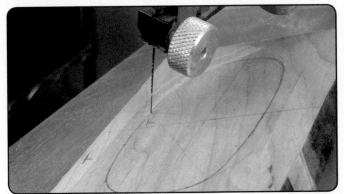

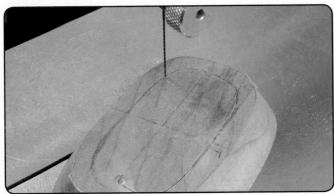

14 **Cut the base.** Center the bowl on the base blank. Trace the outline of the bottom onto the base. Tilt the left side of the saw table down to 30°. Cut along the line in a **counterclockwise** direction to make the outward-flaring base.

15 **Cut a recess in the base.** Draw a ring ⅜" (10mm) in from the edge on the upper (narrower) edge of the base. Drill a vertical blade-entry hole inside the ring and cut along the line with the saw table level (square to the blade).

16 **Make the base top and bottom.** Trace the base onto the thin purpleheart. Invert the base on the other piece of purpleheart and trace the outline. Cut both pieces of purpleheart with a #2 blade.

17 **Assemble the weighted base.** Glue and clamp the bottom edge of the base to the corresponding piece of purpleheart. Weigh the bowl without the base, and then fill the base with your choice of weights, such as BBs, lead sinkers, or lead shot, until it weighs the same as the bowl. Fill the empty spaces in the base with caulk, epoxy, or some other filler to minimize rattling. Glue and clamp the top onto the base, and let it dry.

CUTTING THE SLOT DESIGN

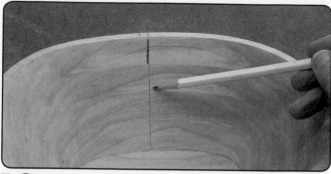

18 **Sand the weighted base.** Sand all of the pieces flush, using a belt sander with the table tilted to 30°. To give the base a smaller flare, set the belt sander tableb square to the belt and sand the lower edge to rough out the desired shape. Smooth the curve with a pad sander.

19 **Draw the guidelines for the slot pattern.** Choose one side of the bowl for the front, and draw a vertical centerline on the inner and outer faces. These centerlines will be used to place the slot pattern.

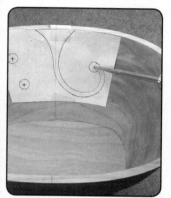

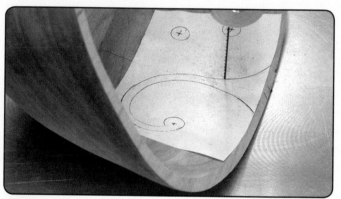

20 **Drill the holes in the sides.** Tape the cutting pattern to the inside face. Align the center marks and pierce the hole centers with an awl. Remove the pattern and set it aside. Drill holes with a ¹⁄₁₆" (2mm)-diameter bit to mark the drilling points on the outside face. Invert the bowl and, using a ³⁄₈" (10mm)-diameter brad-point bit at a downward angle, drill in from the outside until the brad point is visible inside the bowl. Then, drill from the inside out to complete the hole.

21 **Cut the slot.** Reattach the pattern to the inside of the bowl. Start cutting at the top edge of the bowl with a #5 blade. Cut as far as you can, rocking the bowl as needed for greater access. If needed, use a #2/0 spiral blade to complete the cut.

COMPLETING THE PROJECT

22 **Refine the slot area.** Use a rotary tool to enlarge the slot and holes. I use carbide burrs to remove the wood and small sanding drums to smooth the edges. Glue sandpaper to a small dowel to finish sanding the slot. The edges must be completely smooth to avoid snagging the yarn.

23 **Shape the bowl.** Soften and shape the upper edge of the bowl with round inflatable and flexible pad sanders. Be careful not to catch the fretwork section with the round sander sleeve; it will tear the sleeve and may break the wood. Hand-sand the upper edges to remove any remaining rough spots.

24 **Attach the base to the bowl.** Make sure the glue faces of the bowl and base are flat. Place the base on the bowl and check the size and contour; adjust the base as needed. Glue and clamp the base to the bowl. Clean up any glue squeeze-out before the glue sets.

25 **Finish the bowl.** Apply a coat of shellac to seal the wood. When the shellac is dry, buff the finish with 320-grit sandpaper until the wood feels smooth. Apply a coat of beeswax and mineral oil finish with a brush or soft rag. When the finish is dry, buff it to a soft sheen.

Inside Bowl Fretwork Pattern
Copy at 100%

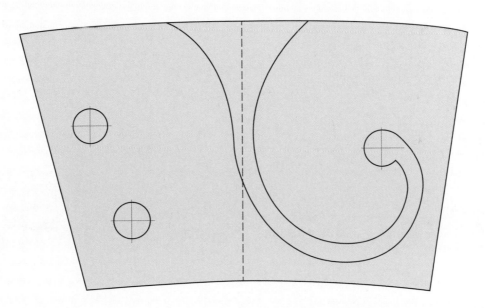

Pattern measures 2 ¹¹⁄₁₆" (68mm)
at the dotted centerline

TEST INCH

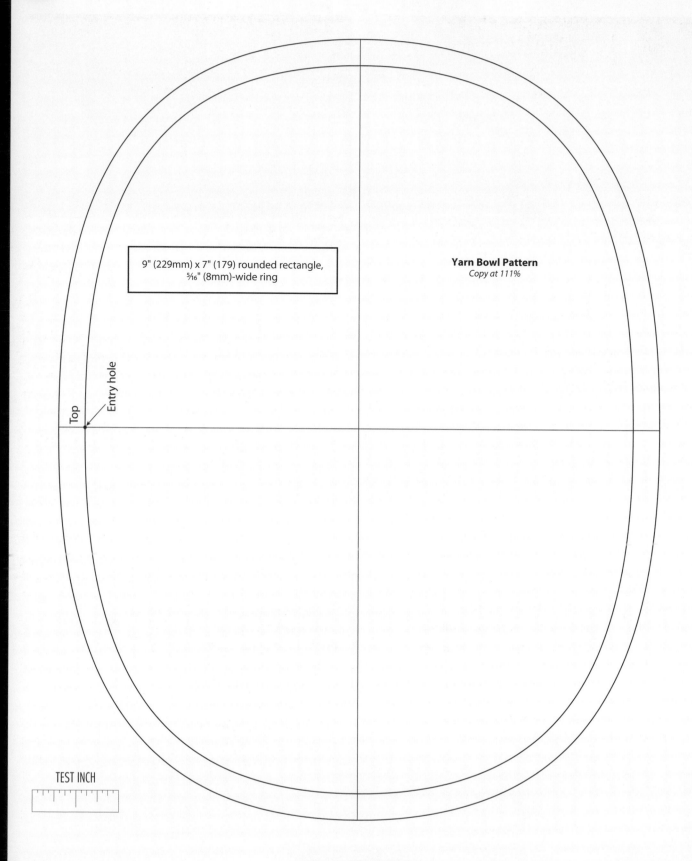

9" (229mm) x 7" (179) rounded rectangle,
⁵⁄₁₆" (8mm)-wide ring

Yarn Bowl Pattern
Copy at 111%

Top

Entry hole

TEST INCH

Oval Scalloped Cypress Bowl: A Step-by-Step Guide

When it comes to bowls, "functional" doesn't have to mean lackluster or boring. The large size of this cypress bowl makes it useful as a breadbasket, while its oval shape and scalloped sides make it an ideal container for ornaments or other decorative objects. Despite its unique appearance, the project requires only familiar tools and techniques. I chose cypress for its attractive grain and ease in cutting and sanding, but any of the softer hardwoods can be used.

Wood

- ¾" (19mm) cypress, 11½" (292mm) x 8½" (216mm)

Materials

- Repositionable adhesive
- Wood glue, Weldbond preferred
- Sleeves for the inflatable sanders: coarse, medium, and fine
- 2" (51mm) scalloped discs for the flexible pad sander, assorted grits
- Sandpaper for hand sanding
- Spray shellac, or clear finish of choice

Tools

- #7 skip-tooth scroll saw blade
- #54 or smaller wire size drill bit
- Shop-made angle guides: 20°, 25°, 30°
- Round inflatable sanders, standard and small sizes
- 2" (51mm) flexible pad sander
- Bowl press, or boards and clamps for gluing
- 12" (305mm) flat tile with 150-grit sandpaper attached

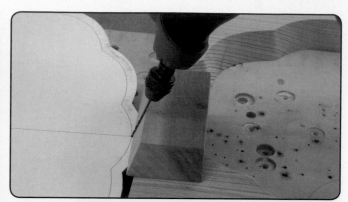

1 **Draw registration lines across the width and length of the blank.** Attach the pattern to the cypress using repositionable adhesive. Tilt the left side of the saw table down to 20°. Cut along the outer line in a clockwise direction.

2 **Use a 20° shop-made angle guide to drill a blade entry hole where indicated on the pattern.** Insert the blade and cut around the line in a clockwise direction to complete the first ring. Remove the pattern, transferring its top mark to the ring and to the blank. Mark the top of each additional ring as it is cut to keep the rings orientated during glue-up.

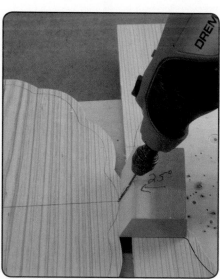

3 **Place the first ring on the blank, matching top marks and registration lines.** Trace the inner edge of the ring to form the cutting line for the second ring. Use a 25° angle guide to drill a blade entry hole on this line, directly opposite the hole drilled for the first ring.

4 Tilt the left side of the saw table down to 25°. Using the top edge as a guide, cut clockwise around the outside of the blank to increase its angle. Be careful not to cut into the top edge. Insert the blade into the entry hole drilled in Step 3 and cut clockwise along the line to complete the second ring.

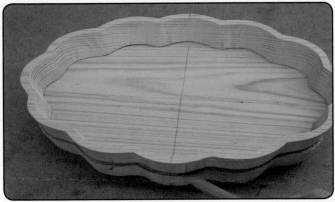

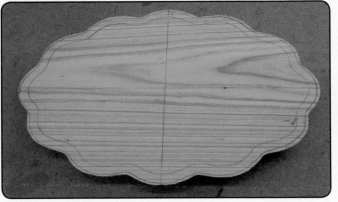

5 Place the second ring on the blank, aligning the top marks and registration lines. Trace the inner and outer edges to form the cutting line for the third ring. Drill a 30° blade entry hole on the inner cutting line, on the same side as the hole drilled for the first ring. Tilt the left side of the saw table down to 30°. Cut along the outer line in a clockwise direction. Insert the blade into the entry hole and cut clockwise to complete the third ring.

6 Place the third ring on the blank, aligning tops and registration lines. Trace the outer edge of the ring to form the cutting line for the base. Tilt the left side of the saw table down to 35°. Cut clockwise along the line to complete the base.

7 Stack the rings with their top marks aligned. Check for spaces between them and correct by sanding with a 150-grit piece of sandpaper attached to a 12" square (305mm) flat tile. Glue the rings together and place in a press.

CHAPTER 4: Multiple-Angle Bowls

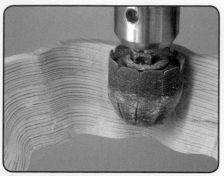 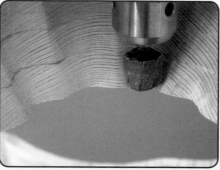 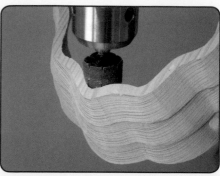

8 **Sand the inside of the rings.** Use the round inflatable sanders chucked into a drill press, and coarse sleeves. Use the larger sander for the upper rings and the smaller one for the bottom ring. Invert the rings to shape the inside of the bottom ring. When the inside is smooth and the scallops are even, use the medium and fine sleeves to refine the surface.

 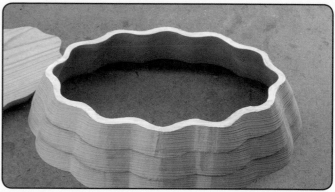

9 **Place the rings on the base, top marks aligned.** Check for spaces and correct any that appear, using the instructions in Step 7. Apply glue to the underside of the third ring and glue on the base. Place the bowl in a press for five minutes, then remove it and clean up any squeeze-out on the surface of the base. Re-clamp the bowl and let it dry thoroughly.

10 **Sand the bowl exterior with a 2" (51mm) flexible pad sander until the surface is smooth and the scallops are even.** Start with a coarse grit and sand progressively through the grits to 220. The top edge should be the same width all around, but not less than ⅛" (3mm). Use the inflatable and pad sanders to correct uneven areas.

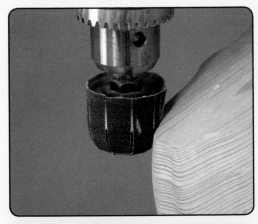

11 Use the large round inflatable with medium and fine sleeves to shape and soften the edge of the base. Use the small round inflatable with medium and fine sleeves to soften the inner and outer edges of the top. Finish by hand sanding, then remove any sanding dust.

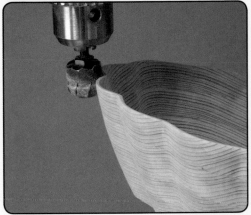

12 Apply a sealer coat of spray shellac. Smooth the surface with 320-grit sandpaper. Finish the bowl with additional coats of shellac or your choice of clear finish, rubbing down between coats with 0000 steel wool as needed.

OVAL SCALLOPED CYPRESS BOWL: A STEP-BY-STEP GUIDE

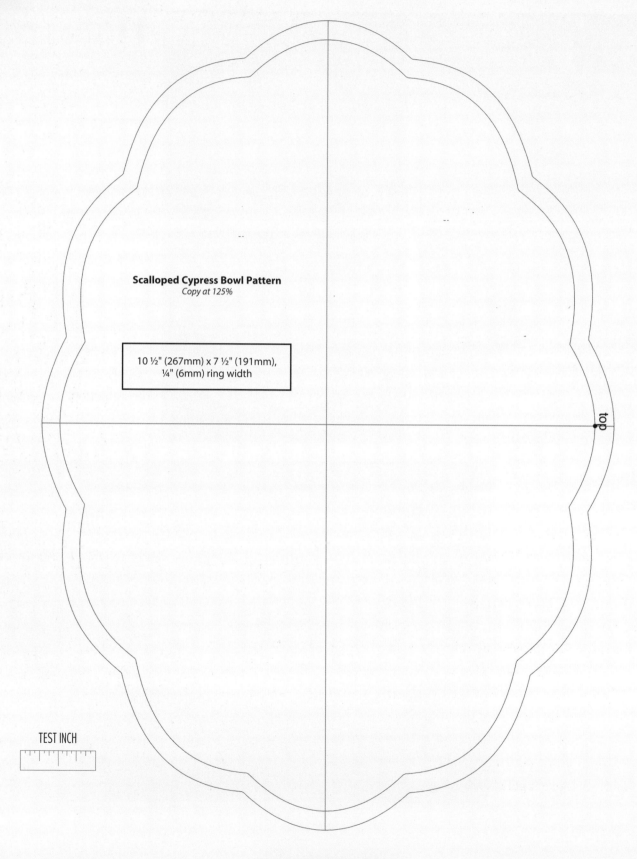

Scalloped Cypress Bowl Pattern
Copy at 125%

10 ½" (267mm) x 7 ½" (191mm),
¼" (6mm) ring width

top

TEST INCH

Ripple-Edged Round Bowl

This dainty round bowl features a rim with ten petal-like flutes. What differentiates this bowl from other petal-shaped bowls in this book is that only the top rim is petal shaped; the rest of the bowl is round. The top shaping is done after the rings are cut. This technique allows you to put a decorative edge on a bowl or vase of any appropriate shape (see Ripple-Edged Vase, page 178). Since the bowl is a small one, the base will be more in proportion if its thickness is reduced slightly by sanding its lower face with a disc or belt sander before it is glued to the rings.

Wood
- (1) 7½" x 7½" x ¾" (191mm x 191mm x 19mm) mahogany

Materials
- Packing tape (optional)
- Glue
- Repositionable adhesive
- Sanding discs for flexible pad sander, assorted grits 60 to 400
- Sandpaper for inflatable ball sander, assorted grits 60 to 320 (optional)
- Sandpaper for hand sanding, assorted grits 220 to 400
- 0000 steel wool or 320-grit sanding sponge
- Spray shellac or Danish oil

Tools
- Scroll saw blade, size #9
- Drill bit size #54 or 1/16" (2mm)
- Awl
- Ruler
- Bowl press or clamps
- 2" (51mm) flexible pad sander
- Inflatable ball sander and pump (optional)

MAKING THE BOWL

1. Draw guidelines on the bowl blank.

2. Glue the bowl pattern to the blank with reposition-able adhesive, using the awl to align the guidelines.

3. Cut the outer circle clockwise at a 30° angle, saw table tilted left side down.

4. Drill an entry hole on the inner circle at 20°.

5. Cut the inner circle at a 20° angle, saw table tilted left side down, cutting clockwise. Remove pattern.

6. Place the completed first ring on the bowl blank. Don't worry if the edge hangs over a bit; it will be sanded smooth when you sand the outside of the bowl. Mark the top and transfer the guidelines.

7. Trace the inner circle to form a cutting line for the second ring.

8. Drill a 20° entry hole for the second ring.

9. Cut the second ring at 20°.

10. Bevel the remaining piece (the base) to 30°, using the upper profile as a guide (see sidebar, Beveling the base, page 104).

11. Glue the petal-shaped pattern (opposite) to the top ring with repositionable adhesive and follow the instructions to create a scalloped edge (see sidebar, Cutting a petal edge on a round bowl, page 105). The ring will look rough after the preliminary sanding. The sanding will be completed after the bowl is glued up.

12. Glue the rings together, clamp, and let dry.

13. Sand the inside of the rings smooth, keeping the inside of the bottom ring round.

14. If desired, reduce the thickness of the base by sanding the underside.

15. Glue the base to the rings, clamp, and let dry.

16. Finish shaping the petals, using the inflatable ball and flexible pad sanders.

17. Sand the outside of the bowl smooth.

18. Apply finish of choice.

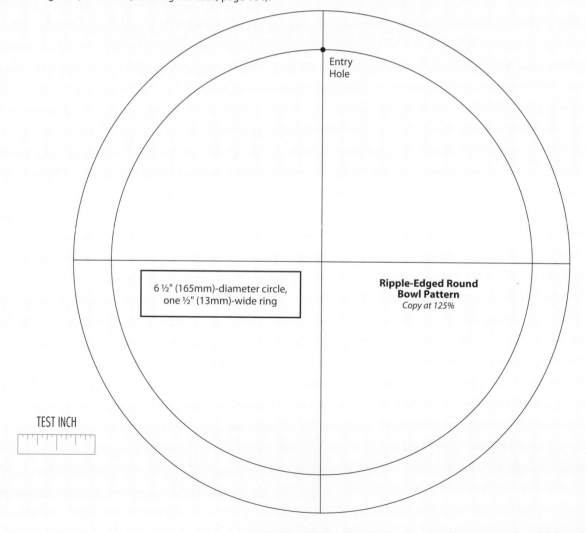

Entry Hole

6 ½" (165mm)-diameter circle,
one ½" (13mm)-wide ring

**Ripple-Edged Round
Bowl Pattern**
Copy at 125%

TEST INCH

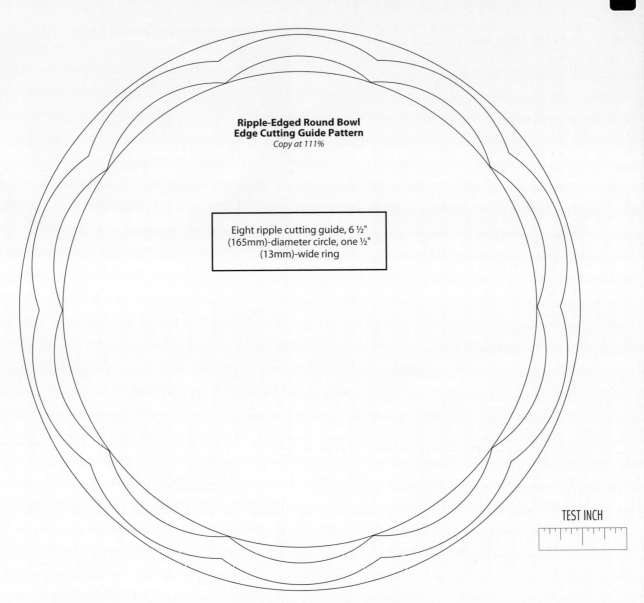

**Ripple-Edged Round Bowl
Edge Cutting Guide Pattern**
Copy at 111%

Eight ripple cutting guide, 6 ½"
(165mm)-diameter circle, one ½"
(13mm)-wide ring

TEST INCH

RIPPLE-EDGED ROUND BOWL

Cutting a petal edge on a round bowl

To get a petal effect on a round bowl, the petals must be cut into the top ring after it has been cut to maintain the roundness of the lower edge. To do this, cuts are made into the inner and outer edges of the ring at angles that do not interfere with the shape of the lower edge. Here's how:

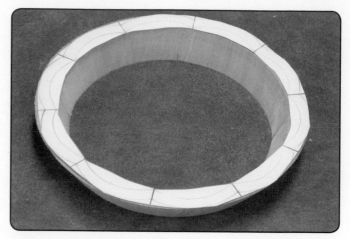

1 Attaching the pattern. Glue the pattern for the petal edge to the top rim with repositionable adhesive.

2 Cutting the outer petals. Tilt the scroll saw table 15°, left side down. Cut clockwise along the outer edge of the pattern.

3 Cutting the inner petals. Tilt the saw table 40°, left side down. Cut clockwise along the inner edge of the pattern. Be careful not to cut into the lower edge of the ring.

4 Sanding the outside. Smooth the outer edge with a spindle sander, table set to 15°.

5 Sanding the inside. Smooth the inner edge with a spindle sander, table set to 40°.

6 **Completing the rough-sanding.** The ring is left rough at this point to avoid damage during glue-up. Final sanding will be done after the bowl is glued together.

Beveling the base

To cut down on the amount of sanding needed to contour the base, excess wood can be removed by using the top profile of the base as a guide to give the base a steeper angle. Once the excess wood is removed, the base is sanded as usual to complete the shaping.

RIPPLE-EDGED ROUND BOWL

Four-Petal Curved Bowl

This gently curved bowl is a variation of the petal bowl, but is somewhat less demanding to cut and shape because of its fewer lobes and wider inner curves. Simple in design, it is ideally suited for wood with an interesting color or grain. For ease in sanding, place entry holes on curved areas, not at points.

Wood
- (1) 8" x 8" x ¾" (203mm x 203mm x 19mm) cherry

Materials
- Packing tape (optional)
- Glue
- Repositionable adhesive
- Sanding discs for flexible pad sander, assorted grits 60 to 400
- Sandpaper for inflatable ball sander, assorted grits 60 to 320 (optional)
- Sandpaper for hand sanding, assorted grits 220 to 400
- 0000 steel wool or 320-grit sanding sponge
- Spray shellac or Danish oil

Tools
- Scroll saw blade, size #9
- Drill bit size #54 or 1/16" (2mm)
- Awl
- Ruler
- Bowl press or clamps
- 2" (51mm) flexible pad sander
- Inflatable ball sander and pump (optional)

MAKING THE BOWL

1. Draw guidelines on the bowl blank.

2. Glue on the pattern with repositionable adhesive, using the awl to center it on the blank.

3. Tilt the scroll saw table to 20°, left side down. Cut clockwise along the outer line.

4. Drill a 20° entry hole on the inner line and cut to complete first ring. Remove pattern.

5. Place the ring on the blank. Mark the top and transfer the guidelines from the blank.

6. Trace the inside of the first ring to form the cutting line for the second ring.

7. Drill a 25° entry hole on the second ring and cut clockwise with the saw table tilted 25°, left side down.

8. Place the second ring on the blank, mark the top, and transfer the guidelines. Trace the inside of the second ring to form the cutting line for the third ring.

9. Drill a 35° entry hole and cut the third ring clockwise, table tilted 35°, left side down.

10. Glue up the rings, clamp, and let dry.

11. Sand the inside of the rings smooth.

12. Glue on the base, clamp, and let dry.

13. Contour the base to obtain a nicely rounded shape.

14. Sand the outside of the bowl smooth.

15. Apply finish of choice.

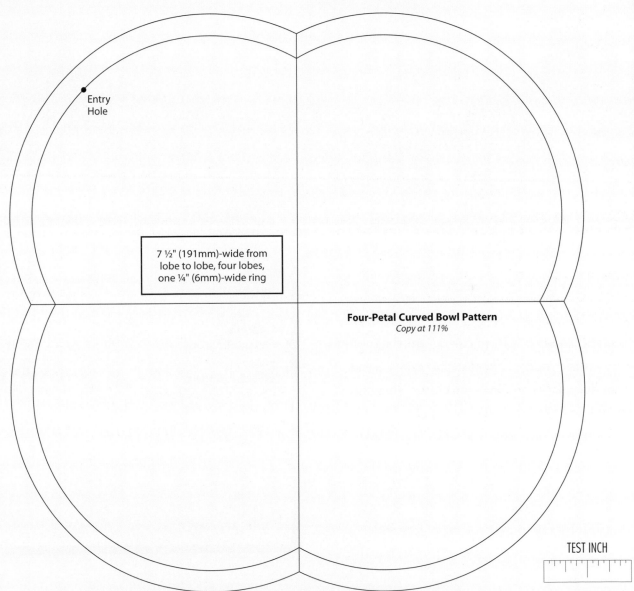

Entry Hole

7 ½" (191mm)-wide from lobe to lobe, four lobes, one ¼" (6mm)-wide ring

Four-Petal Curved Bowl Pattern
Copy at 111%

TEST INCH

FOUR-PETAL CURVED BOWL

Heart-Shaped Bowl

This delicate curved bowl is the perfect gift for an engagement or anniversary. I used a light-colored piece of poplar with a pretty grain, but most any wood should work. To facilitate sanding, place entry holes on flat or curved surfaces only, not at top or bottom points. Once glued up, the bottom can be sanded aggressively to create a nicely curved shape, but check carefully as you sand to keep the bowl symmetrical.

Wood
- (1) 8" x 8" x ¾" (203mm x 203mm x 19mm) poplar

Materials
- Packing tape (optional)
- Glue
- Repositionable adhesive
- Sanding discs for flexible pad sander, assorted grits 60 to 400
- Sandpaper for inflatable ball sander, assorted grits 60 to 320 (optional)
- Sandpaper for hand sanding, assorted grits 220 to 400
- 0000 steel wool or 320-grit sanding sponge
- Spray shellac or Danish oil

Tools
- Scroll saw blade, size #9
- Drill bit size #54 or 1/16" (2mm)
- Awl
- Ruler
- Bowl press or clamps
- 2" (51mm) flexible pad sander
- Inflatable ball sander and pump (optional)

MAKING THE BOWL

1. Draw guidelines on the bowl blank.

2. Glue the pattern to the wood with repositionable adhesive, aligning the guidelines.

3. Cut the outline at 20°, saw table tilted left side down, cutting clockwise.

4. Drill an entry hole on the inside of the first ring at 20° and complete the cutting of the first ring. Remove the pattern.

5. Place the first ring on the bowl blank.

6. Transfer the guidelines and trace the outline for second ring.

7. Drill an entry hole at 25° for the second ring.

8. Cut the ring at 25°, saw table left side down, cutting clockwise.

9. Place the second ring on the bowl blank and transfer the guidelines.

10. Trace the outline for the third ring.

11. Drill an entry hole at 35° for the third ring.

12. Cut the ring at 35°, saw table left side down, cutting clockwise.

13. Glue the rings together, clamp, and let dry.

14. Sand the inside of the rings smooth.

15. Glue on the base, clamp the bowl, and let it dry.

16. Contour the base as desired.

17. Sand the outside of the bowl smooth.

18. Apply finish of choice.

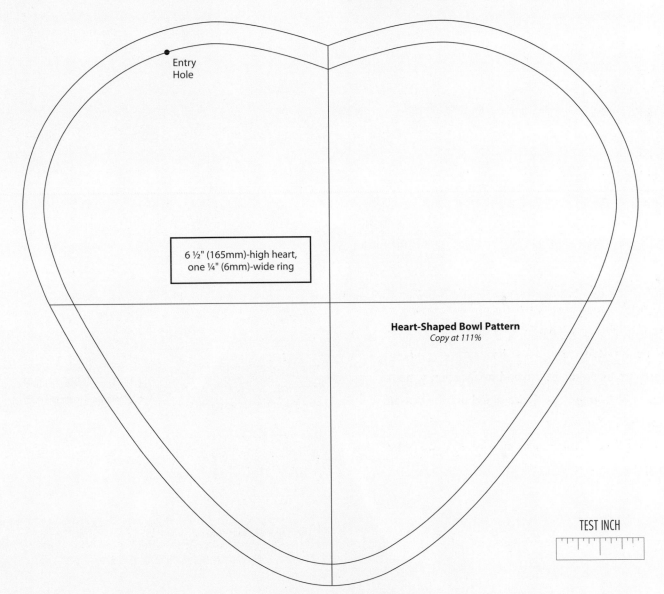

Entry Hole

6 ½" (165mm)-high heart, one ¼" (6mm)-wide ring

Heart-Shaped Bowl Pattern
Copy at 111%

TEST INCH

HEART-SHAPED BOWL

CHAPTER 5

Bowls created from thin stock—less than ¾" (19mm)—require a steeper cutting angle.

Thin Wood Bowls

Graceful, delicate bowls can be crafted from thinner stock. This chapter features bowls made from wood that is less than ¾" (19mm) thick. The construction principles are the same as for bowls made from thicker wood, but a steeper cutting angle is required for the same ring width. Thin wood bowls are a natural for colorful laminations, or for showcasing beautifully grained pieces of wood that might be too challenging to use as thicker stock.

Eight-Segment Bowl: A Step-by-Step Guide

This multi-segment bowl is made from thin pieces of purpleheart and mahogany, although any two contrasting woods will work. The lamination is somewhat time consuming, but once completed, the bowl cuts quickly and easily, and looks as though you spent many hours gluing scores of pieces together. Two easy-to-make jigs help the task go more smoothly. The semicircle construction method lets you use narrow pieces of stock, which you are likely to have on hand as leftovers from other projects.

Wood
- (2) 8" x 4" x ¼" (203mm x 102mm x 6mm) purpleheart
- (2) 8" x 4" x ¼" (203mm x 102mm x 6mm) mahogany
- Scrap of ¼" (6mm) purpleheart (optional)

Materials
- Packing tape (optional)
- Double-sided tape
- Glue
- Repositionable adhesive
- Sanding discs for flexible pad sander, assorted grits 60 to 400
- Sandpaper for inflatable ball sander, assorted grits 60 to 320 (optional)
- Sandpaper for hand sanding, assorted grits 220 to 400

- 0000 steel wool or 320-grit sanding sponge
- Spray shellac or Danish oil

Tools
- Scroll saw blade, size #9
- Drill bit size #54 or 1/16" (2mm)
- Awl
- Ruler
- Compass
- Bowl press or clamps
- Clamps for lamination
- 2" (51mm) flexible pad sander
- Inflatable ball sander and pump (optional)
- ½" (13mm) drill bit and ½" (13mm) plug cutter (optional)
- Gluing jig (recommended)
- Alignment jig (recommended)

LAMINATION GUIDE

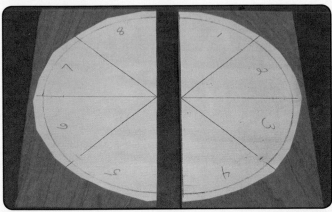

1 Prepare the wood. Attach one piece of mahogany to one piece of purpleheart with double-sided tape. Place the tape so that the pieces will hold together after the circle is cut. Repeat for the other pieces of mahogany and purpleheart. Cut the lamination guide in half and glue one half to each piece of taped wood with repositionable adhesive.

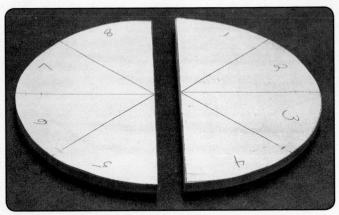

2 Cut the perimeter. Cut out the perimeter of the pattern for each piece.

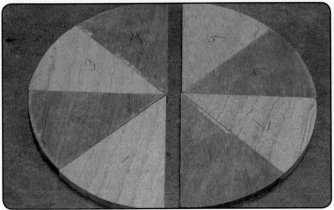

3 Cut the segments. Cut along the lines to divide each piece into four segments. Remove the pattern from each segment. Separate the segments and write the number from the pattern on both top and bottom pieces. Assemble segments to make four semicircles, alternating colors and keeping the numbers in order.

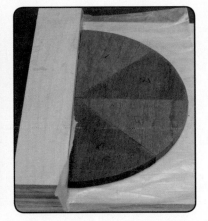

4 Glue the semicircles. Glue up each semicircle using the alignment jig (see sidebar on page 115). Place waxed paper between the wood and the jig to prevent sticking. Use finger pressure to clamp the segments together. Press the segments against the strip of wood to get a flat edge. Let dry.

5 Complete the circles. Glue each semicircle to its mating half to form two complete circles. You may need to sand the straight edges before gluing if they are not perfectly flat. Be sure the numbers on the wedges go in order for each circle. Clamp each circle in the gluing jig (see sidebar on page 114) to get a good join. Let dry.

6 Complete the lamination. Stack the circles so that the numbers on the top and bottom segments are the same and the colors alternate. Make an alignment mark on the outside edge so you can reposition the pieces properly when gluing up. Erase all other marks and sand all faces smooth. Place one circle on waxed paper on the plywood circle from the gluing jig. Spread glue evenly over the surface. Place the other circle on top, using the mark on the edge to align it properly. Cover with waxed paper, clamp tightly, and let dry overnight. Bowl press shown on its side for illustrative purposes.

EIGHT-SEGMENT BOWL: A STEP-BY-STEP GUIDE

TEST INCH

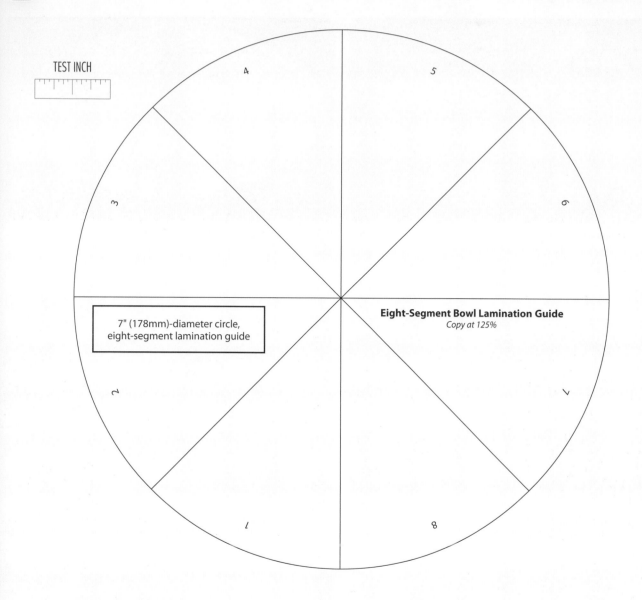

4   5

3   6

7" (178mm)-diameter circle,
eight-segment lamination guide

Eight-Segment Bowl Lamination Guide
Copy at 125%

2   7

1   8

Gluing jig

Materials
- (1) 12" x 7½" x ¾" (305mm x 191mm x 19mm) plywood

This simple jig makes it easier to clamp the semicircles when you glue them to each other. Cut a 7½" (191mm) circle out of the center of the plywood. Use the sidepieces to apply clamping pressure to the semicircles when you glue them together, and the center circle for extra height in the bowl press.

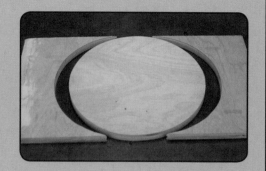

MAKING THE BOWL

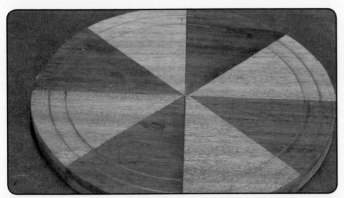

1 Marking the first ring. Draw two intersecting guidelines on the bowl blank. Place the point of your compass in the center and draw a circle that is 6½" (165mm) in diameter. This is the outer cutting line for the first ring. Make a mark on a guideline that is 3⁄8" (10mm) inside that circle. Use your compass to draw a smaller circle that forms the inside edge of the first ring.

2 Cutting the outer profile. Tilt the saw table 38°, left side down. Cut clockwise along the outer circle. Mark the top.

3 Drilling the first entry hole. Drill an entry hole on the inner ring at a 38° angle using an angle guide or a drill press with a tilting table.

4 Completing the first ring. Insert the blade into the entry hole and cut along the inner line to complete the first ring. Mark the top.

5 Marking the second ring. Place the first ring on the bowl blank, aligning the tops, and trace the inside of the first ring on the blank. This is the cutting line for the second ring. You do not need to make additional marks since the lamination pattern will guide the alignment when gluing the bowl together.

Alignment jig

Materials
- (1) 8½" x 8½" x ½" (216mm x 216mm x 13mm) plywood
- (1) 8½" x 1½" x ¾" (216mm x 38mm x 19mm) plywood or hardwood

This quickly made jig provides support for the segments as you glue up the semicircles. To make the jig, glue the hardwood strip to the edge of the plywood. Clamp and let dry.

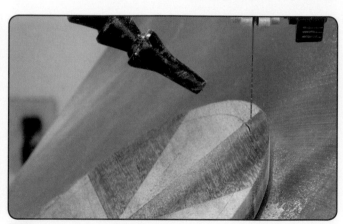

6 **Drilling the second ring entry hole.** Drill an entry hole for the second ring on the opposite side from the first entry hole. Avoid placing entry holes back to back on the same ring.

7 **Cutting the second ring.** Insert the blade in the second entry hole and cut out the second ring. Mark the top.

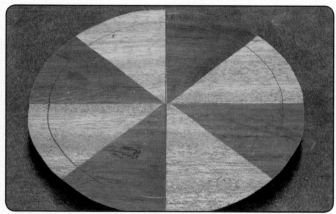

8 **Marking the third ring.** Place the second ring on the bowl blank, aligning the tops. Trace the inside of the second ring on the bowl blank. This is the cutting line for the third ring.

9 **Cutting the third ring.** Drill an entry hole for the third ring, cut and mark as for the second ring.

10 **Stacking and checking for spaces.** Stack the rings, aligning the tops. Check for spaces between the rings and sand if necessary. Remove any pencil marks from the face of the rings.

11 **Gluing the rings.** Glue up the rings, aligning the top marks and laminations, and clamp. Do not glue on the base at this time. If using the bowl press, do not over-tighten, since this could distort the laminated rings. Remove the bowl after a few minutes and clean off excess glue. Reclamp the bowl and let dry.

12 **Sanding the inside of the bowl.** Sand the inside of the bowl smooth using a spindle sander, flexible sanding pad, or inflatable sanding ball. Work from coarser to finer grits.

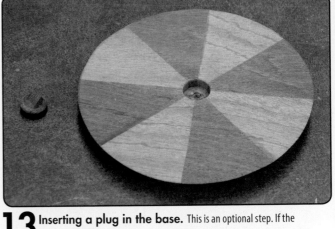

13 **Inserting a plug in the base.** This is an optional step. If the segments don't meet evenly in the center, or if you want a more decorative effect, cut a ½" (13mm)-diameter plug of purpleheart from a scrap of ¼" (6mm) stock. Drill a ½" (13mm)-diameter hole in the center of the bowl base, slightly less than ¼" (6mm)-deep and glue the plug into place. Sand flush.

14 **Gluing on the base.** Glue on the base, keeping the top aligned with the rings. If you've used the plug, be sure it is centered. Clamp glued up bowl and let dry.

15 **Sanding the outside and contouring.** Sand the outside of the bowl smooth, working from coarser to finer grits. Contour the upper and lower edges.

Alternate version

To make the alternate version of this bowl, you will need to make the following changes to the materials and instructions:

- Materials and bowl size are the same
- Ring width is ¼" (6mm) instead of ⅜" (10mm)
- Cutting angle is 28° instead of 38°
- Five rings are cut instead of three

16 **Finishing the bowl.** Apply mineral spirits to the bowl to reveal any glue spots. Mark them with a white pencil or chalk. When dry, sand off the glue spots. Apply the first coat of shellac and let dry. Smooth the surface with a 320-grit sanding sponge or 0000 steel wool. Vacuum, remove any remaining particles with a damp cloth or paper towel, and then recoat. Repeat until the desired finish is obtained.

Dizzy Bowl: A Step-by-Step Guide

Like most woodworkers, my shop is cluttered with colorful wood scraps I can't bear to throw away. While some shapes come in handy, thin, narrow strips never seem right for whatever project I'm starting. However, the day I discovered what woodturners call "dizzy bowls," I knew I'd found a home for my ever-increasing pile of strips. These segmented bowls are laminated in such a way that they create intricate and colorful designs.

Materials
- Scrap wood: ⅜" (1cm) thick x 9½" (24.1cm) long, in sufficient quantity to build two matching blanks
- Thick PVA wood glue, such as Weldbond or Quick&Thick
- Spray adhesive: repositionable
- Sandpaper
- Grit sleeves: round, for inflatable sander
- Spray shellac or lacquer
- Steel wool: 0000

Tools
- Sanders: drum sander (recommended), belt with tilting table, round inflatable
- Clamps or shop-made gluing jig and silicon mat
- Scroll saw blades: #7 reverse-tooth
- Drill or rotary tool with #54 wire size bit
- Shop-made 45° angle drilling guide
- Press for gluing, or clamps and boards
- Compass
- Awl

Choosing the wood

Everyone has different scraps in their pile, so every dizzy bowl looks different. Experiment with your scraps to find a pleasing combination. To create a bowl with a distinct center stripe like mine, you'll need an odd number of strips (I used 27 per blank) in sufficient quantity to create two identical blanks, each about 9½" (24.1cm) square. So you can see how the blank looked before I cut it, I've included a photo and listed my selections and their widths at right.

1 Maple, ⅞" (2.2cm)

2 Oak, ⅜" (1cm)

3 Maple, ½" (1.3cm)

4 Oak, ⅜" (1cm)

5 Yellowheart, ⅛" (3mm)

6 Padauk, ½" (1.3cm)

7 Yellowheart, ⅛" (3mm)

8 Oak, ⅜" (1cm)

9 Maple, ½" (1.3cm)

10 Padauk, ¼" (6mm)

11 Black veneer, N/A

12 Yellowheart, ¼" (6mm)

13 Black veneer, N/A

14 Padauk, ½" (1.3cm)

Gluing up a dizzy bowl blank

Most woodturners glue up one thick blank that they resaw to form two or more thin blanks. Because I started with thin strips, I substituted two identical thin blanks for the single resawn one.

You can cut the strips with either a scroll saw or table saw; just make sure the edges you plan to glue together are smooth and straight. The starting thickness of my strips was about ⅜" (1cm). When the glue-up was dry, I sanded each blank to ¼" (6mm) thick and then cut it into a circle. Rotated and glued together, the circles form a single ½" (1.3cm)-thick blank from which I cut the bowl.

CHAPTER 5: Thin Wood Bowls

using a jig

using clamps

Two ways to glue

For this project, you need to glue thin strips of wood together and keep them relatively flat. Otherwise, you'll be losing a lot of wood to sanding. There are two ways to accomplish that: use a jig or use clamps.

Using a simple gluing jig

Attach two strips of wood to a piece of MDF in an L shape. Make sure one piece is longer than your bowl strips. Place a nonstick surface, such as a silicon mat or waxed paper, on the jig. Apply glue to one edge of the first strip. With that strip flat on the mat, press the mating edge of the next strip firmly against it. Slide the strips together to spread the glue evenly, and then press the strips firmly against the side of the jig until the glue sets up. Add additional strips, one at a time, in the same manner. Glue the strips in sections for better control. Repeat for the second blank. Let the glue dry thoroughly.

Using clamps

Choose a board narrower than your strips are long and line it with waxed paper. Arrange the strips on the board and glue them in sections, following the instructions above. Clamp the sides as shown. Make sure that the gluing surfaces meet fully and the glued-up strips don't cup. Then, glue the sections together.

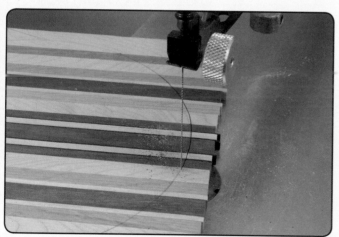

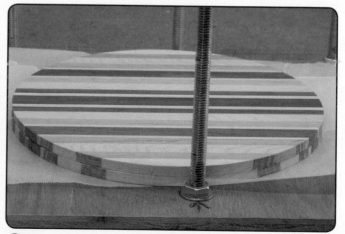

1 **Glue the strips together (see Two Ways to Glue, above).** Sand each blank to a uniform ¼" (6mm) thickness. I use a drum sander. Using a compass and identical center points, draw an 8½" (21.6cm)-diameter circle on each blank. Cut each circle with the saw table level. Place the circles together, matching centers and stripes. Rotate the circles slightly to establish an attractive pattern and mark that position on the edges.

2 **Glue the two circles together in the rotated position.** Use the marks, and then clamp the two together and let the glue dry. Check the thickness. If the blank is more than ½" (1.3cm) thick, sand wood evenly from both faces to reduce it to ½" (1.3cm) thick.

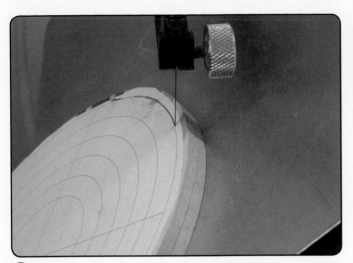

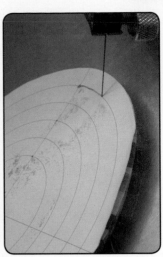

3 **Mark the center of the blank.** Attach the cutting pattern to the blank with repositionable adhesive, using an awl to make sure the centers are aligned. Tilt the left side of the saw table down to 45° and cut clockwise around the outside of the first ring. Support the blank as you cut to keep it from sliding down and distorting the cutting angle.

4 **Drill blade-entry holes at a 45° angle where indicated on the pattern.** Use a shop-made angle guide (see Tip on page 122), and angle the holes toward the center of the circle. Insert the blade and cut clockwise to complete the first ring. Mark the top of the ring. Cut and mark the remaining four rings in the same way.

GLUING THE RINGS

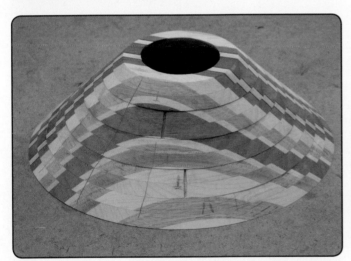

5 **Stack the rings, rotating them to continue the pattern.** Mark the alignment on the inner and outer faces. Check for spaces between rings and sand the problematic surfaces until the rings lie flat against each other.

6 **Glue the rings in stages.** This keeps them from slipping out of alignment. Glue the top two rings together. Clamp them, let them dry about 10 minutes, and then add the next ring. Repeat until you have glued all of the rings. Do not glue on the base yet. Let the glue dry thoroughly.

SANDING AND FINISHING THE PROJECT

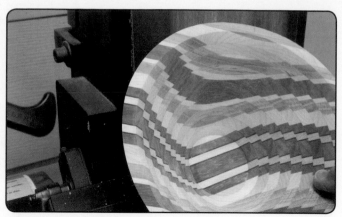

7 Sand the inside of the bowl. Use a round inflatable sander. Start with a coarse sleeve to remove the blade and burn marks, and any other irregularities. Then, progress to medium- and fine-grit sleeves. Make sure the bottom edge of the smallest ring is sanded into a smooth, regular circle.

8 Place the rings on the base. Rotate the base to select the most attractive orientation for the inside and outside of the bowl. Mark its position and glue the base to the lower rings, removing it briefly from the clamps to clean up any squeeze-out before it dries. When the glue has dried completely, tilt the table of a vertical belt sander to 45° and sand the bowl exterior smooth.

9 Sand the outside of the bowl. Use progressively finer sandpaper up to 220 grit. Remove any scratch marks left by the belt sander. Soften the inside and outside edges with the round inflatable sander, finishing by hand. Apply several coats of spray shellac or lacquer, rubbing between coats with 0000 steel wool.

Shop-made angle guide

Make a drilling guide for blade entry holes by cutting a scrap block of wood on a scroll saw, table saw, or miter saw at any desired angle for the project at hand. The Dizzy Bowl requires a 45° angle.

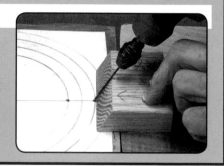

Dizzy Bowl Pattern
Copy at 125%

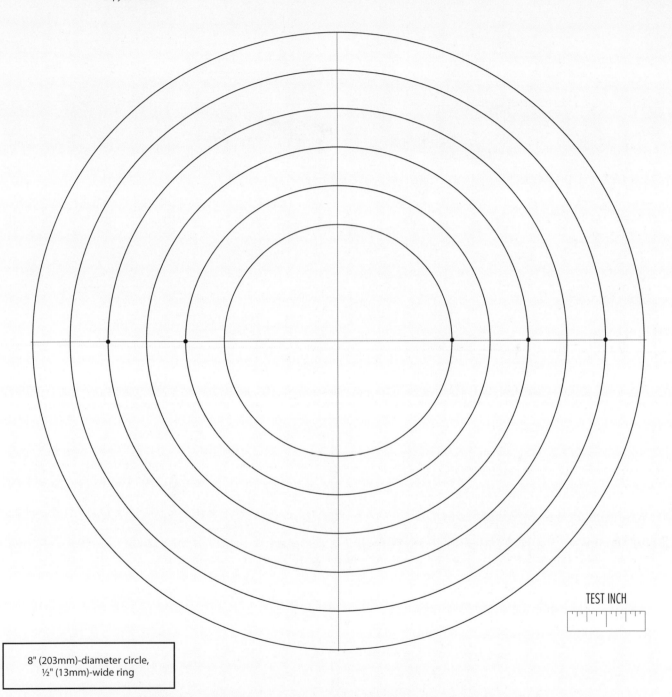

8" (203mm)-diameter circle,
½" (13mm)-wide ring

TEST INCH

DIZZY BOWL: A STEP-BY-STEP GUIDE

Open-Segmented Oval Bowl: A Step-by-Step Guide

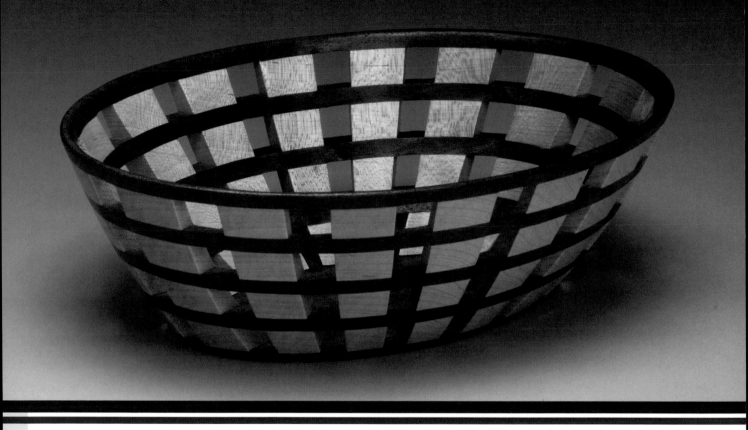

Scrolled bowls may vary in shape but typically have solid sides. Lathe-turned bowls may have open-segmented sides but are typically round. This bowl combines an oval shape with open segmentation; its construction will confound even experienced woodworkers. The key is a blank consisting of wedges glued to an oval substrate. When the blank is cut into rings, the wedges form a pattern of slices and spaces that is virtually indistinguishable from the open segmentation of a lathe-turned bowl.

Wood

- (2) ½" (13mm) x 4" (102mm) x 10½" (267mm) maple
- (1) ¼" (6mm) x 7½" (191mm) x 10½" (267mm) sapele
- (1) ¼" (6mm) x 5¼" (133mm) x 7¼" (184mm) sapele for bottom piece

Materials

- Repositionable adhesive
- Wood glue, Weldbond preferred
- Sandpaper, assorted grits
- 0000 steel wool
- Gloss spray lacquer
- Sleeves for round inflatable sanders: coarse, medium, and fine grits
- Discs for flexible pad sander, assorted grits

Tools

- Vertical belt sander
- Scroll saw blades, #5 or #7, #3
- Drill bits, #54 or #56 wire size, #62 or smaller wire size
- Bowl press, or boards and clamps for gluing
- Awl
- Shop-made angle guides: 25°, 30°, 35°, 40°
- Sandpaper attached to a 12" (305mm) square flat tile
- Large round inflatable sander
- Small round inflatable sander
- 2" (51mm) or 3" (76mm) flexible pad sander
- 2" (51mm) round sanding mop, 180- and 220-grit
- 4" (102mm) 320-grit sanding mop

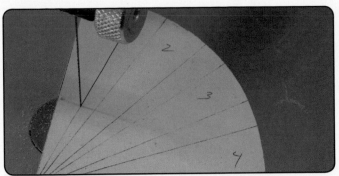

1 **Cut the segment pattern in half by cutting along the cut line.** Using repositionable adhesive, attach each half to a piece of maple 10½" (267mm) long, aligning the straight edge of the pattern with the long edge of the wood. Using a #5 or #7 blade, cut around the perimeter of each pattern, then cut along the straight lines to create a total of sixteen numbered segments. Remove the pattern from each segment, transferring its number to the wood.

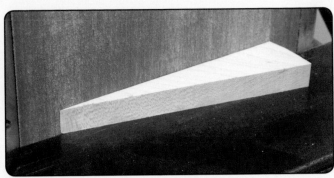

2 **Use a belt sander to sand the sides of the segments just until smooth.** The outer curves of all segments should be approximately equal in length.

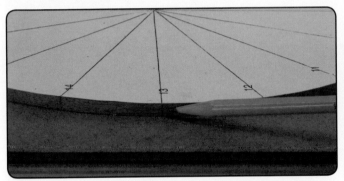

3 **Use repositionable adhesive to attach the layout pattern to the 10½" (267mm) piece of sapele.** Cut around the circumference with a #3 blade to form an oval. Mark the ends of the segment lines on the sides of the oval to create reference marks for positioning the segments. Drill a tiny (#62 or smaller wire size) through hole at the center point. Remove the pattern and set aside to use in Step 5.

4 **Connect the marks made in Step 3.** Do this by drawing eight lines that run through the center of the blank. These form the reference lines you'll use in Steps 5 and 6.

5 **Place each segment on its corresponding line.** Use the pattern from Step 3 as a guide. Center the curved edge of each segment on its corresponding mark and place its front point on the reference line. Mark the center point of the curved edge of each segment. Remove all segments except numbers 1, 5, 9, and 13. These will be glued on first to anchor the spacing.

6 **Apply glue to the bottom of each of the four segments.** Press each firmly into place, positioning it as in Step 5. Remove any squeeze-out with a toothpick. Place the unit in a press until the glue is set. Glue and clamp the remaining twelve segments in the same manner, working one quarter at a time. Be sure to keep the spaces between segments even. When all segments are glued, clamp the unit and let the glue dry fully.

OPEN-SEGMENTED OVAL BOWL: A STEP-BY-STEP GUIDE

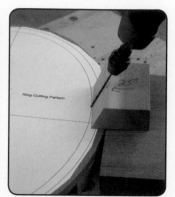

7 **Place the blank with the sapele side facing up.** Draw two intersecting registration lines, using the marks on the edge of the sapele at segments 1, 5, 9, and 13. Attach the ring cutting pattern to the sapele with repositionable adhesive, matching the registration lines and using an awl to match the center points.

8 **Use an awl to mark the drilling point for the blade entry hole.** This is indicated on the pattern, and should fall between the segments. Use a shop-made angle guide and #54 bit to drill a 25° entry hole at that point. Tilt the left side of the saw table down to 20° and cut the outer oval in a clockwise direction. Then, tilt the left side of the saw table down to 25°. Insert the blade into the drilled entry hole and cut the inner oval in a clockwise direction to complete the first ring. Mark the tops of the ring and the blank.

Angle guides for a curved-sided bowl

Drilling guides are essential for making accurate blade entry holes at steep angles. To make a guide, cut one edge of a small block of hardwood to the desired angle, then true that edge with a belt or disc sander set to that same angle. This project requires four angle guides: 25°, 30°, 35°, and 40°.

9 **Place the ring on the blank, matching tops.** Use a sharp pencil to mark the inner edge of each segment. Remove the ring and connect the segments to form a continuous cutting line for the second ring. Drill a 30° blade entry hole between the segments, across from the first hole. Tilt the left side of the saw table down to 30° and cut the second ring. Repeat the same procedure for the third and fourth rings, drilling and cutting at 35° for the third ring and 40° for the fourth ring. Each ring will be wider at the bottom than the preceding one.

10 **Remove "fuzzies" from segment edges by hand sanding.** Use a sheet of 150-grit sandpaper attached to a 12" (305mm) square tile to smooth and clean the top and bottom faces of the rings. Stack them in an inverted position with tops and rings aligned. Draw reference lines down the sides in several locations around the bowl to help you position the rings during glue-up.

11 **Apply glue to the underside of the segments of the first ring.** Keep glue away from the side edges to minimize squeeze-out between the segments. Place the ring with its segments facing upward. Place the second ring on top. Use the reference lines for alignment, then press down firmly. Use a toothpick to remove squeeze-out between the segments. Repeat with the third and fourth rings. Place the assembly in a press, right side up. Place the remainder of the blank in the center to stabilize the bottom ring; make sure that area is free of glue. Clamp the assembly; use just enough pressure to establish a firm bond or the segments might collapse. If squeeze-out appears between segments, remove it with a toothpick or long skewer. Try to do this without removing the bowl from the press. Keep the assembly clamped until the glue dries completely.

12 **Sand the inside of the upper three rings.** Use the large round inflatable sander and a coarse sleeve. Use short brushing strokes and angle the rings so that only the top and center areas of the sleeve contact the wood. This keeps the slotted bottom area of the sleeve from snagging on the segment edges. Be careful not to gouge the wood between the segments as you sand. When the upper three rings are smooth and free of excess glue, change to the small round inflatable sander. Use a coarse grit sleeve to sand the bottom ring, and to spot sand the upper rings if needed. Invert the assembly to shape the lower edge of the end segments. When the interior has been shaped, repeat the process with medium grit sleeves.

CHAPTER 5: Thin Wood Bowls

OPEN-SEGMENTED OVAL BOWL: A STEP-BY-STEP GUIDE

13 Complete the sanding of the inside with 2" (51mm) round sanding mops in grits 180 and 220. You can also use the fine sleeve of the small round inflatable, but be careful not to gouge the wood between segments. Alternatively, you can complete the sanding by hand.

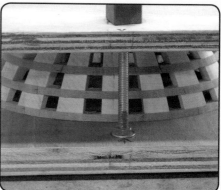

14 Trace the outside of the bottom ring on the remaining piece of sapele. Tilt the left side of the saw table down to 40°. Cut the outline in a clockwise direction to create the base. Apply glue to the underside of the segments of the bottom ring and clamp the bowl in a press. Exert just enough clamping pressure for a firm bond. Remove the bowl briefly after five minutes to clean away any squeeze-out between segments and on the surface of the base, then re-clamp and let the glue dry completely.

16 Sand the exterior with a 2" (51mm) or 3" (76mm) flexible pad sander. Work progressively through the grits to 220. Be sure that the top rim is smooth and evenly thick around the bowl, and correct as needed. Use the upper part of the large round inflatable to soften and shape the inner and outer upper edges. Finish sanding by hand, then apply several coats of clear spray lacquer, buffing between coats with 0000 steel wool or a well-worn 320-grit sanding mop, as needed.

15 Tilt the table of the belt sander to 40°. Sand the edge of the base until it is continuous with the segments of the bottom ring.

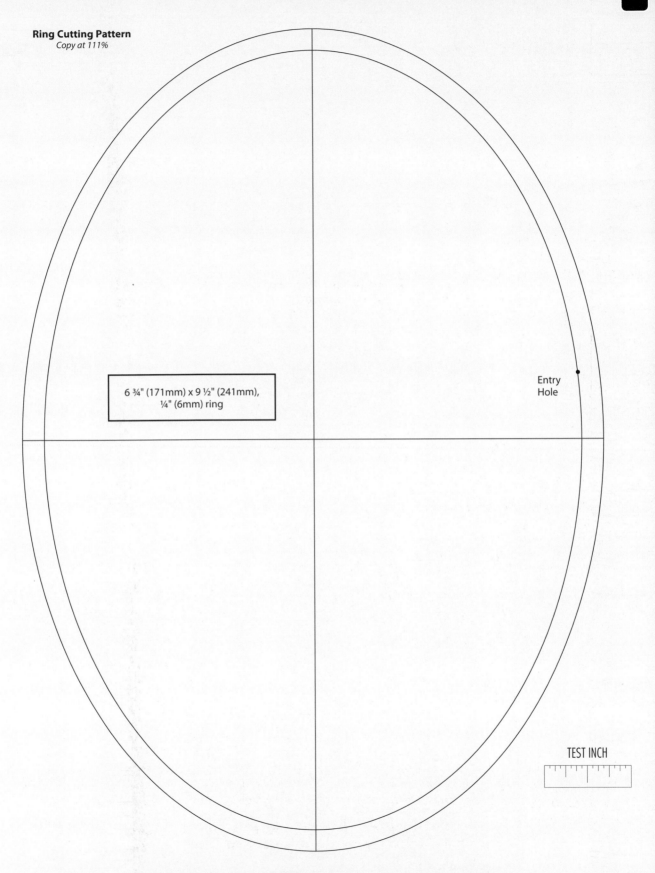

Ring Cutting Pattern
Copy at 111%

6 ¾" (171mm) x 9 ½" (241mm),
¼" (6mm) ring

Entry
Hole

TEST INCH

OPEN-SEGMENTED OVAL BOWL: A STEP-BY-STEP GUIDE

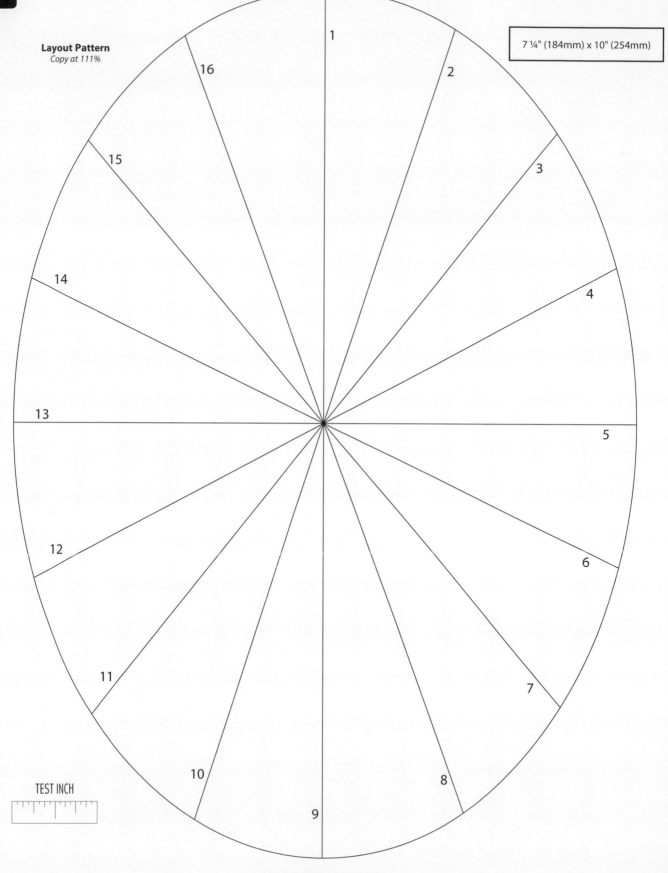

Layout Pattern
Copy at 111%

7 ¼" (184mm) x 10" (254mm)

TEST INCH

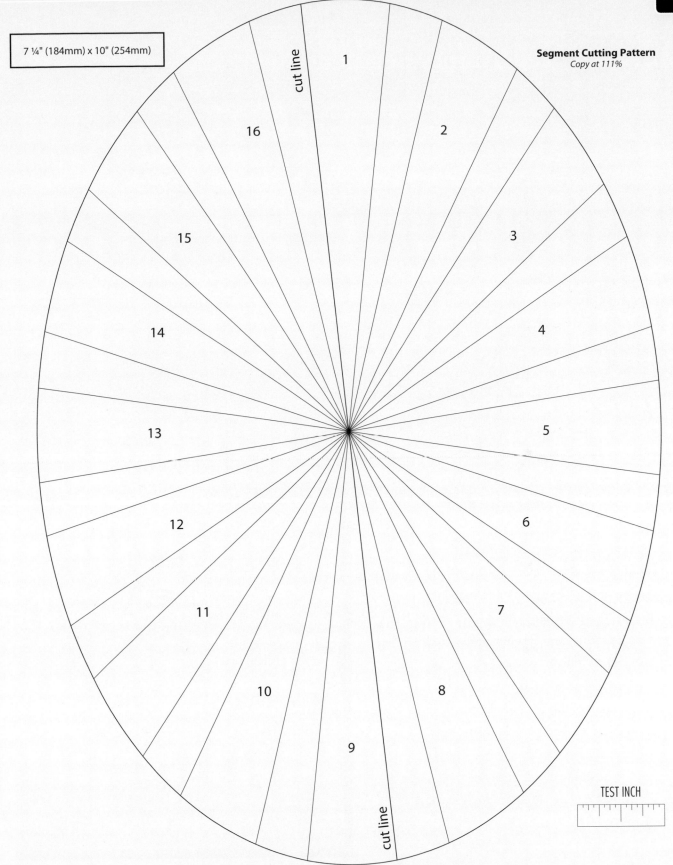

7 ¼" (184mm) x 10" (254mm)

Segment Cutting Pattern
Copy at 111%

cut line

1

16

2

15

3

14

4

13

5

12

6

11

7

10

8

9

cut line

TEST INCH

OPEN-SEGMENTED OVAL BOWL: A STEP-BY-STEP GUIDE

Multi-Colored Twenty-Segment Bowl

This colorful bowl is made from two circles, each containing twenty segments. Like the Eight-Segment Bowl (page 112), it is formed from semicircles glued together to form full circles. However, to produce a swirl effect these circles are rotated when glued together.

The use of so many little pieces poses both organizational and gluing challenges. Numbering each segment when removing the pattern easily solves the organizational challenge. The gluing challenge is solved by use of an alignment jig (see sidebar on page 115) to keep them in place.

Wood

- (2) 8" x 4" x ¼" (203mm x 102mm x 6mm) purpleheart
- (2) 8" x 4" x ¼" (203mm x 102mm x 6mm) yellowheart
- Scrap of ½" (13mm) purpleheart for center plug

Materials

- Packing tape (optional)
- Glue
- Repositionable adhesive
- Double-sided tape
- Sanding discs for flexible pad sander, assorted grits 60 to 400
- Sandpaper for inflatable ball sander, assorted grits 60 to 320 (optional)
- Sandpaper for hand sanding, assorted grits 220 to 400
- 0000 steel wool or 320-grit sanding sponge
- Spray shellac or Danish oil

Tools

- Scroll saw blade, size #9
- Drill bit size #54 or ¹⁄₁₆" (2mm)
- Awl
- Ruler
- Compass
- Bowl press or clamps
- Clamps for lamination
- 2" (51mm) flexible pad sander
- Inflatable ball sander and pump (optional)
- ½" (13mm) drill bit and ½" (13mm) plug cutter
- Gluing jig (recommended, see page 114)
- Alignment jig (recommended, see page 115)

LAMINATION GUIDE

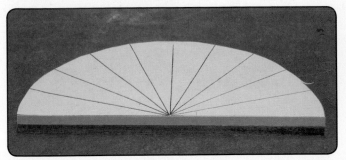

1 Prepare the wood. Attach one piece of yellowheart and one piece of purpleheart with double-sided tape. Place the tape so that the pieces will hold together after the outer circle is cut. Repeat for the other pieces of yellowheart and purpleheart. Cut a lamination guide pattern (page 134) in half and glue one half to each piece of taped wood with repositionable adhesive. Cut along the curved line for each piece to form a semicircle.

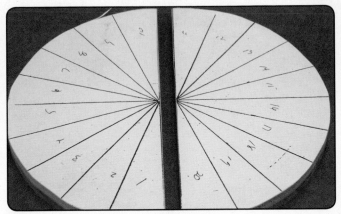

2 Number the segments. Number the segments 1–10 on the first piece, 11–20 on the second piece.

3 Cut the segments. Cut along the lines to divide each piece into ten segments. Separate the matching pieces and number each lower piece the same as its matching upper piece. Assemble the pieces to make four semicircles. The pieces should align easily. However, if you are having trouble obtaining a tight fit because the ends of some of the segments are too long and won't lie flat, sand a little off those ends. Although this will result in a small space in the center, the plug that is inserted later will ensure a finished look.

4 Glue up the semicircles. Glue up each semicircle using the gluing jig. Place waxed paper underneath to prevent wood from sticking to the jig. Press the pieces together firmly, then let dry. No clamping is necessary.

5 Glue the semicircles together. Glue each semicircle to its matching half to form two complete circles. Be sure the numbers on the wedges go in order for each circle. Use the gluing jig to get a good join, and let dry.

6 Glue the circles together. Stack the circles so that the numbers on the top and bottom segments match. Rotate the top circle half a segment. Draw an alignment mark on the outside edge. Erase all other pencil marks and sand the faces smooth. Place waxed paper on the plywood circle from the gluing jig. Place one circle on top. Spread glue evenly over the surface. Place the other circle on top, matching alignment marks. Cover with waxed paper, clamp, and let dry overnight.

MULTI-COLORED TWENTY-SEGMENT BOWL

MAKING THE BOWL

1. Draw guidelines on the blank.

2. Attach the cutting pattern (opposite) to the blank with repositionable adhesive. Use the awl to center the pattern on the lamination.

3. Tilt the saw table 28°, left side down.

4. Cut along the bowl outline, cutting clockwise. Mark the top on the outer rim.

5. Drill 28° entry holes, alternating sides, and cut out five rings.

6. Mark the top of each ring.

7. Stack the rings, rotating every other ring one segment to continue the spiral.

8. Check for spaces between rings. Sand if needed.

9. Glue the rings, clamp, and let dry.

10. Sand the inside of the bowl smooth.

11. Cut a ½" (13mm) plug from the scrap of purpleheart.

12. Drill a ½" (13mm) hole through the center of the base.

13. Glue the plug into place. Sand the base smooth.

14. Glue on the base, making sure the plug is centered. Clamp and let dry.

15. Sand the outside of the bowl.

16. Apply finish of choice.

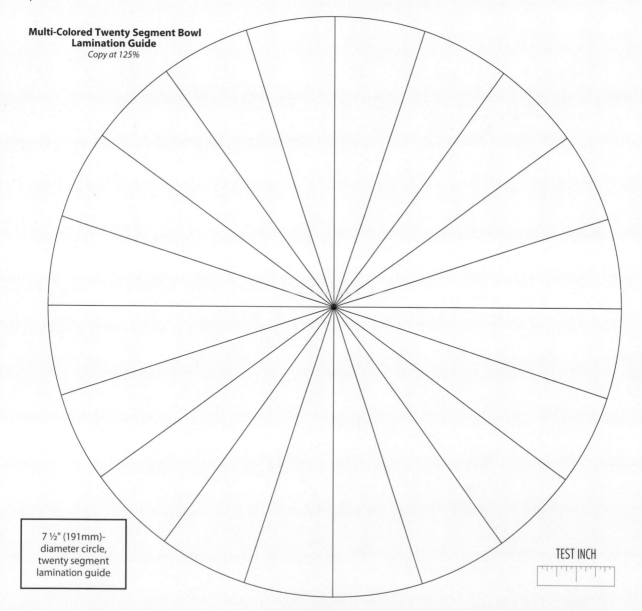

Multi-Colored Twenty Segment Bowl Lamination Guide
Copy at 125%

7 ½" (191mm)-diameter circle, twenty segment lamination guide

TEST INCH

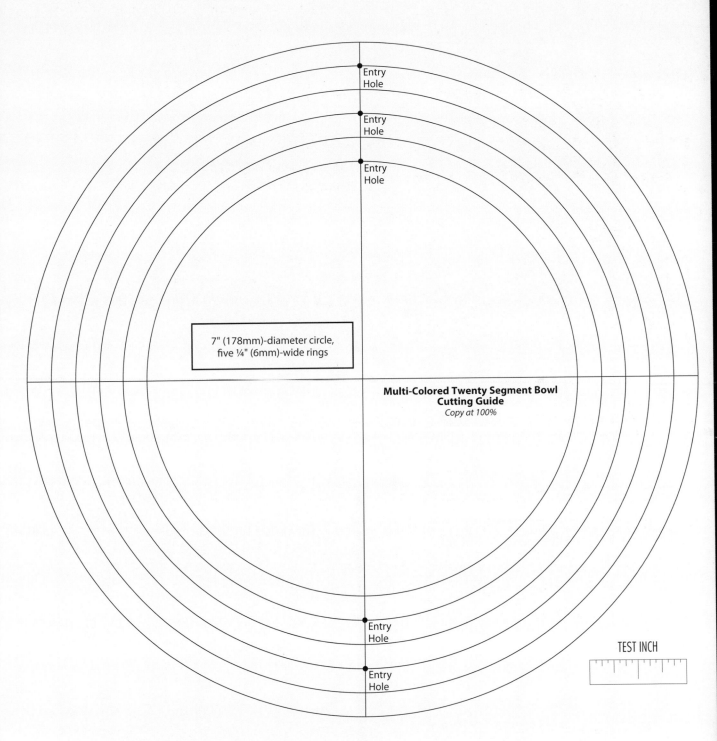

Entry
Hole

Entry
Hole

Entry
Hole

7" (178mm)-diameter circle,
five ¼" (6mm)-wide rings

**Multi-Colored Twenty Segment Bowl
Cutting Guide**
Copy at 100%

Entry
Hole

Entry
Hole

TEST INCH

MULTI-COLORED TWENTY-SEGMENT BOWL

Seven-Lobe Ripple-Edged Bowl

Certain colors evoke specific images. This combination of oak, padauk, and walnut creates a fall palette, reminiscent of changing leaves. For a spring effect, I might have used yellowheart, purpleheart, and maple. The ripple edge adds additional interest with little extra effort.

I cut the bowl blank to a circle before gluing up the pieces to allow the use of the bowl press. I've found that thin woods tend to warp unless clamped securely, and that the best way to counteract that is with the even pressure the bowl press provides. If you are not using a bowl press, glue up the squares of wood, clamp conventionally, and proceed directly to making the bowl.

Wood
- (1) 7½" x 7½" x 1/8" (191mm x 191mm x 3mm) oak
- (1) 7½" x 7½" x ¼" (191mm x 191mm x 6mm) walnut
- (1) 7½" x 7½" x 1/8" (191mm x 191mm x 3mm) padauk

Materials
- Packing tape (optional)
- Glue
- Double-sided tape (if using a bowl press for the lamination)
- Repositionable adhesive
- Sanding discs for flexible pad sander, assorted grits 60 to 400
- Sandpaper for inflatable ball sander, assorted grits 60 to 320 (optional)
- Sandpaper for hand sanding, assorted grits 220 to 400
- 0000 steel wool or 320-grit sanding sponge
- Spray shellac or Danish oil

Tools
- Scroll saw blade, size #9
- Drill bit size #54 or 1/16" (2mm)
- Awl
- Ruler
- Compass
- Bowl press or clamps
- 2" (51mm) flexible pad sander
- Inflatable ball sander and pump (optional)

LAMINATION GUIDE

1. Stack the wood, using double-sided tape at corners.

2. Using the compass, draw a circle 7½" (191mm) in diameter on the wood.

3. Cut along the circle through all three pieces of wood. Separate.

Remove any tape stuck to the wood.

4. Glue up the wood circles (oak, walnut, then padauk), clamp, and let dry. Keep the grain of all pieces running in the same direction.

MAKING A BOWL

1. Draw guidelines on the laminated blank, padauk side up.

2. Glue the pattern to the blank with repositionable adhesive, aligning guidelines.

3. Cut the outline at 28°, table left side down, cutting clockwise.

4. Drill a 28° entry hole. Complete the first ring, mark the top, and remove the pattern. Place the ring on the blank and transfer guidelines to the ring.

5. Use the first ring to mark the second ring.

6. Drill an entry hole and cut the second ring.

7. Use the second ring to mark the third ring.

8. Cut the third ring.

9. Glue up the rings, clamp, and let dry.

10. Sand the inside smooth.

11. Glue on the base, clamp, and let dry.

12. Sand the outside of the bowl and contour the upper rim.

13. Apply finish of choice.

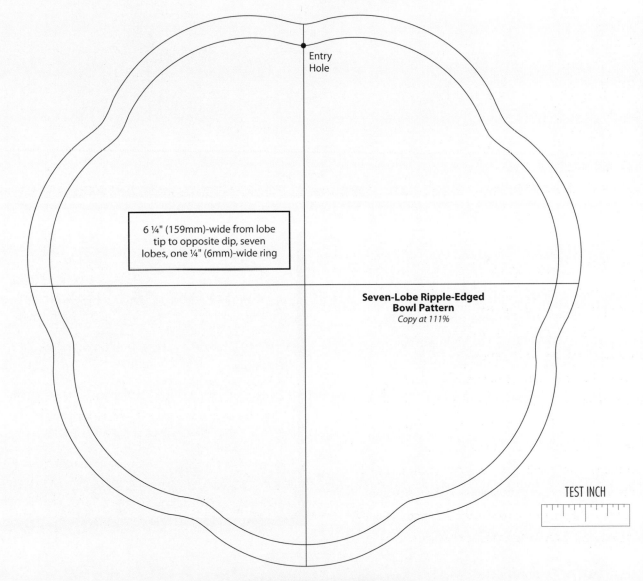

Entry Hole

6 ¼" (159mm)-wide from lobe tip to opposite dip, seven lobes, one ¼" (6mm)-wide ring

Seven-Lobe Ripple-Edged Bowl Pattern
Copy at 111%

TEST INCH

SEVEN-LOBE RIPPLE-EDGED BOWL

Center Lamination Bowl

This straight-sided rectangular bowl has thin walls that give it a delicate look. I chose a darker-colored wood for the center strip, but you can vary the color scheme to your preference. A Danish oil finish was used to highlight the functional appearance of this useful little bowl.

Wood
- (2) 8" x 3" x 5/8" (203mm x 76mm x 16mm) oak
- (1) 8" x 2" x 5/8" (203mm x 51mm x 16mm) Santos mahogany
- (2) 8" x 5/8" x 1/8" (203mm x 16mm x 3mm) maple

Materials
- Packing tape (optional)
- Glue
- Repositionable adhesive
- Sanding discs for flexible pad sander, assorted grits 60 to 400
- Sandpaper for inflatable ball sander, assorted grits 60 to 320 (optional)
- Sandpaper for hand sanding, assorted grits 220 to 400
- 0000 steel wool or 320-grit sanding sponge
- Spray shellac or Danish oil

Tools
- Scroll saw blade, size #9
- Drill bit size #54 or 1/16" (2mm)
- Awl
- Ruler
- Bowl press or clamps
- Clamps for lamination
- 2" (51mm) flexible pad sander
- Inflatable ball sander and pump (optional)

LAMINATION GUIDE

1. Glue up the wood strips in the following order: oak, maple, mahogany, maple, oak. It's a good idea to clamp an additional piece of wood across the lamination to keep the blank flat. Clamp and let dry.

MAKING A BOWL

1. Draw guidelines on the bowl blank.

2. Attach the pattern with repositionable adhesive, using an awl to center it on the guidelines.

3. Tilt the saw table to 23°, left side down.

4. Cut along the outer ring, cutting clockwise.

5. Drill a 23° entry hole and cut along the inner ring to complete the first ring. Remove the pattern.

6. Place the first ring on the blank and mark the top and guidelines on the ring.

7. Trace the outline for the second ring.

8. Drill an entry hole and cut the second ring.

9. Place the second ring on the blank and mark the top and guidelines on the ring.

10. Trace the outline for the third ring.

11. Drill an entry hole and cut the third ring.

12. Stack the rings and check for alignment and spaces.

13. Glue the rings, clamp, and let dry.

14. Sand the inside of the bowl smooth.

15. Glue on the base, clamp, and let dry.

16. Sand the outside of the bowl smooth.

17. Apply finish of choice.

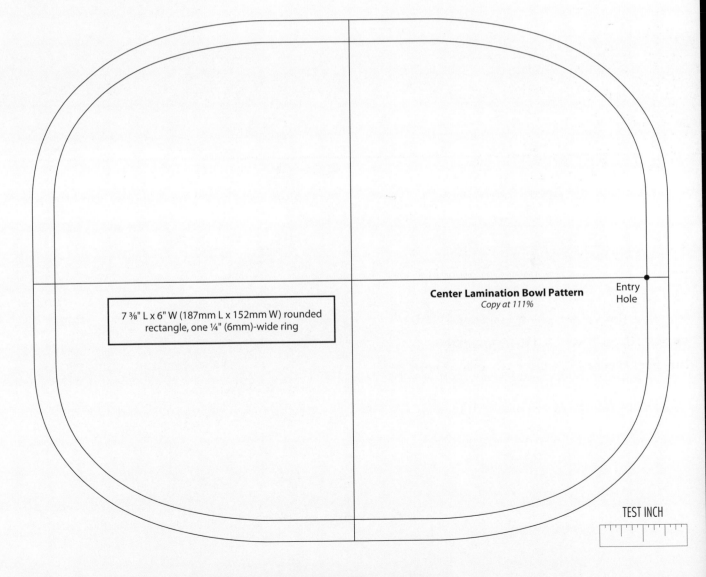

7 ⅜" L x 6" W (187mm L x 152mm W) rounded rectangle, one ¼" (6mm)-wide ring

Center Lamination Bowl Pattern
Copy at 111%

Entry Hole

TEST INCH

CENTER LAMINATION BOWL

Many types of projects other than bowls can be created with the stacked ring method.

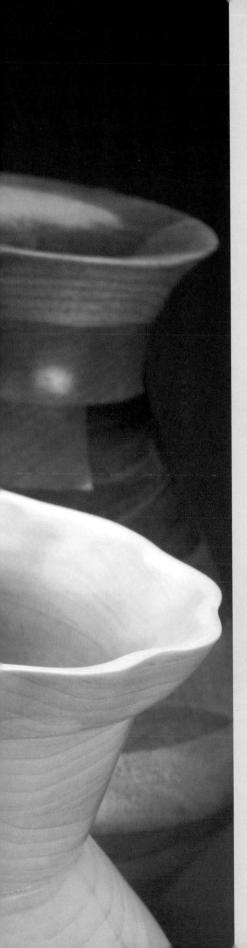

Thinking Outside the Bowl

While a great deal of variety can be achieved using a single set of rings, a whole world opens up when you add additional sets. Two straight bowls stacked top to top become a modern vase, a curved bowl stacked on a straight one becomes a ginger jar, and a straight ring glued to an angled one becomes a base for a candy dish. Ring sets can be of the same or contrasting woods. Plain or laminated blanks can be used. Rings of different thicknesses can be inserted. This chapter explores some of the possibilities that emerge when you think "outside the bowl."

Double-Swirl Vase: A Step-by-Step Guide

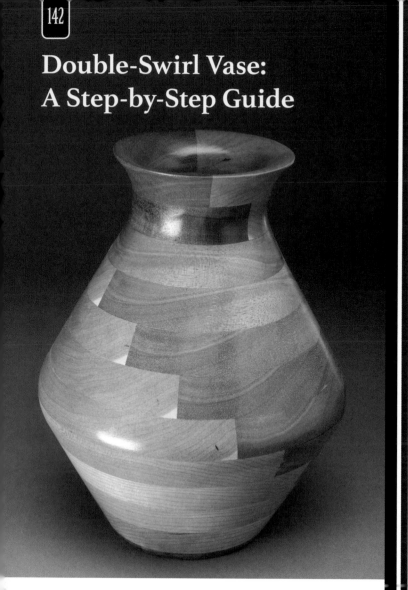

Wood

VASE BODY:
- (1) 8" x 8" x ¾" (203mm x 203mm x 19mm) cherry
- (1) 8" x 8" x ¾" (203mm x 203mm x 19mm) mahogany

BASE:
- (1) 5" x 2½" x ¼" (127mm x 64mm x 6mm) mahogany
- (1) 5" x 2½" x ¼" (127mm x 64mm x 6mm) cherry

NECK:
- (1) 4" x 2" x ¾" (102mm x 51mm x 19mm) mahogany
- (1) 4" x 2" x ¾" (102mm x 51mm x 19mm) cherry

Materials

- Packing tape (optional)
- Glue
- Repositionable adhesive
- Sanding discs for flexible pad sander, assorted grits 60 to 400
- Sandpaper for inflatable ball sander, assorted grits 60 to 320
- Sandpaper for hand sanding, assorted grits 220 to 400
- 0000 steel wool or 320-grit sanding sponge
- Spray shellac or Danish oil

Tools

- Scroll saw blade, size #9
- Drill bit size #54 or 1/16" (2mm)
- Awl
- Ruler
- Compass
- Clamps for lamination
- Bowl press or clamps
- 2" (51mm) flexible pad sander
- Inflatable ball sander and pump

This easy-to-make vase is a good introduction to projects constructed from multiple sets of rings. It consists of two sets of straight-sided rings glued together and topped with a set of rings that have been shaped with both spindle and inflatable ball sanders. I suspected cherry and mahogany would provide an attractive contrast; the flecks of sapwood that appeared in the cherry were an unexpected bonus.

LAMINATION GUIDE

1. Cut the 8" (203mm) pieces of mahogany and cherry in half, cutting along the grain. Number the pieces as shown (right). These pieces will form the vase body lamination.

2. Create two multi-color 8" x 8" (203mm x 203mm) laminated blanks for the vase body by gluing the edges of pieces 1 and 2 together, and the edges of pieces 3 and 4 together. Clamp them and let dry.

3. Mark the top of each blank and sand flat if needed.

4. Glue together the 5" x 2½" x ¼" (127mm x 64mm x 6mm) pieces of cherry and mahogany to make a 5" x 5" x ¼" (127mm x 127mm x 6mm) lamination for the vase base. Rub the edges together to obtain a good bond. Let dry.

5. Glue together the 4" x 2" x ¾" (102mm x 51mm x 19mm) pieces of cherry and mahogany to make a 4" x 4" x ¾" (102mm x 102mm x 19mm) lamination for the vase neck. Clamp and let dry.

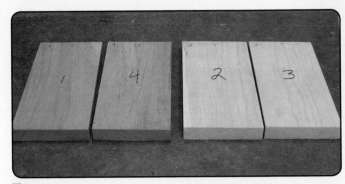

1 **Prepare the wood** for the vase body lamination.

Keeping laminations flat

To keep larger laminations flat as they dry, clamp a piece of wood across the lamination. Be sure to use waxed paper under the cross piece to prevent it from sticking to the lamination.

Entry Hole

Double-Swirl Vase Pattern
Copy at 125%
(Make two copies)

7" (178mm)-diameter circle, one ⅜" (10mm)-wide ring

TEST INCH

DOUBLE-SWIRL VASE: A STEP-BY-STEP GUIDE

MAKING THE VASE

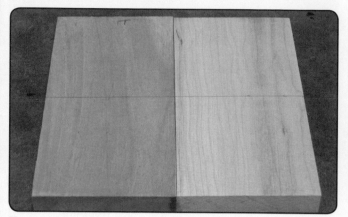

1 Drawing the guidelines on the blanks for the vase body. Mark the midpoints of the sides of each 8" x 8" (203mm x 203mm) laminated blank and draw lines to form intersecting guidelines.

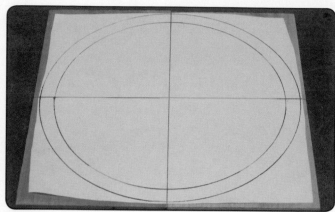

2 Gluing on the vase body pattern. Glue on a vase body pattern with repositionable adhesive to each of the two blanks, using an awl to center the pattern. Align the guidelines on the pattern and the wood. Mark the top.

3 Cutting the outer profile of the vase body. Tilt the saw table 28°, left side down. Cut the profile of both blanks clockwise along the outer line.

4 Marking the top. Mark the tops of both body pieces. As you continue, be sure to mark each ring set clearly—mark all of one set with a number 1, and the other with a number 2.

Note: Because the bowls that form the body of the vase are identical to the Basic Bowl in Chapter 2, page 24, you can use that pattern (page 29) to cut the four rings instead of using the ring method, if you prefer.

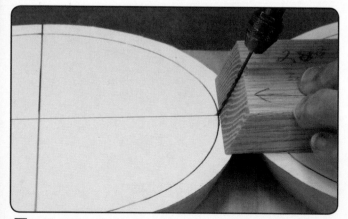

5 Drilling the entry holes in the first ring. Using a tilting drill press or 28° angle guide, drill entry holes on the inner ring for both blanks at a 28° angle.

6 **Completing the first vase body ring.** Insert the saw blade into the entry hole and cut clockwise along the line to complete the ring. Mark the top of the ring. Repeat for the second vase body blank. Remove the patterns.

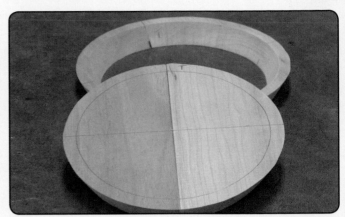

7 **Drawing the second vase body rings.** Place the first ring on the blank and transfer the guidelines from the blank to the sides of the ring and mark the top. Holding the ring in place, trace the inside of the ring on the blank to use as a cutting line for the second ring. Repeat for the second vase body blank.

8 **Drilling the second entry hole.** Mark a point on the second ring opposite the first entry hole. Drill an entry hole at a 28° angle. Repeat for the second vase body blank.

9 **Cutting the remaining rings.** Cut out and mark the second ring for both vase body blanks. Cut out and mark the third and fourth rings for both blanks in the same manner. Be sure to keep each ring set clearly marked.

10 **Preparing the rings for gluing.** Stack each set of rings in a spiral pattern and check for spaces between the rings. Sand as needed. Remove any pencil marks from the lower inner edges and top surfaces of the rings.

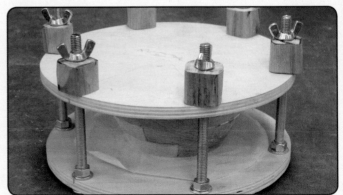

11 **Gluing the rings.** For each set, glue the four rings together, keeping the spiral pattern even. Clamp and let dry. You will have one piece left over from each set of rings. Be sure to mark which piece belongs to each set. These two pieces will be used to form the top assembly in Steps 17–24.

DOUBLE-SWIRL VASE: A STEP-BY-STEP GUIDE

12 **Sanding the inside of the rings.** Sand the inside of each set of rings just until ridges are smoothed out. They do not need to be finely sanded. Use either a flexible pad or inflatable ball sander, or a spindle sander with the table tilted to 28°. Be sure to leave the rings at least ¼" (6mm)-wide at the top and bottom edges to have enough wood for gluing and shaping.

13 **Sanding the outside of the rings.** Sand the outside of each set of rings until any ridges are smoothed out. You will complete the sanding later. You can use either a vertical sander with the table set to 28° or a flexible pad sander. Be sure to leave the rings at least ¼" (6mm)-wide at the top and bottom edges to have enough wood for gluing and shaping.

14 **Cutting the base.** Decide which set of rings to use for the lower half of the vase body. Center that set of rings on the glued-up base lamination. Trace the outline of the bottom ring onto the base piece. Tilt the scroll saw table to 28°, left side down, and cut the base clockwise on that line. Cut generously to the outside of the line.

15 **Gluing on the base.** Glue the base to the bottom of the ring set whose outline you traced. Be sure to continue the spiral pattern. Clamp and let dry. Sand the base flush with the sides.

16 **Completing the body of the vase.** Invert the set of rings without the base (now called the top set) on the set with the base (now called the bottom set). Be sure to continue the spiral pattern. Glue together and weight down. Let dry.

17 **Marking the neck.** For this step, use the leftover piece from Step 11 that belongs to the top set of rings. (The other piece will be used in Step 21.) Place this piece, larger side up, on the laminated piece for the neck, aligning the laminations. Trace the outline.

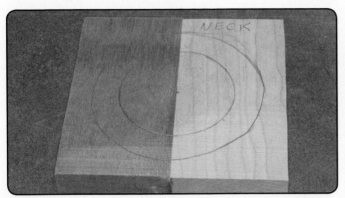

18 **Cutting the neck.** Mark the center of the circle you drew in Step 17. Using a compass, place the point on this center mark and draw a circle that is 1" (25mm) smaller than this circle. This will give you a ring that is about ½" (13mm) wide. With the saw table level, cut along the outer line. Drill a straight entry hole just inside the inner line and cut out the center. Discard the center.

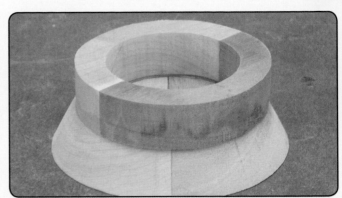

19 **Marking the lower part of the top assembly.** Place the angled piece used in Step 17 so the larger face is down. Center the neckpiece on top of the angled piece and trace the inner circle. This is the cutting line.

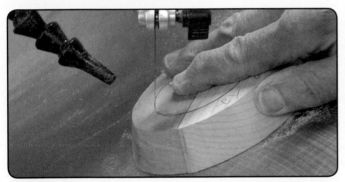

20 **Cutting the lower part of the top assembly.** Drill an entry hole about ¼" (6mm) inside the cutting line at 28°, angled toward the outside of the piece. Tilt the scroll saw table 28°, left side down. Insert the saw blade and cut counterclockwise along the line. This piece is the lower part of the top assembly.

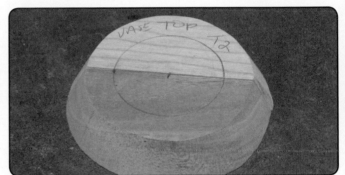

21 **Cutting the upper part of the top assembly.** Repeat Steps 19 and 20 with the remaining piece from Step 11. This piece will be the upper part of the top assembly.

22 **Gluing the top assembly.** Glue together the lower part of the top assembly, the neckpiece, and the upper part of the top assembly, continuing the spiral. Clamp and let dry.

23 **Shaping the top assembly.** Using the spindle sander, smooth the center hole of the neckpiece, and then turn the top assembly on its side to sand in a curved shape.

CHAPTER 6: Thinking Outside the Bowl

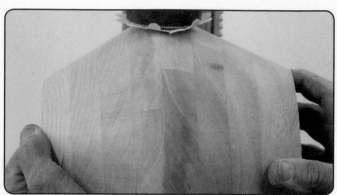

24 **Contouring the top assembly.** Using the inflatable ball sander, smooth the inside join with the neckpiece and contour and thin the upper rim.

25 **Rough-shaping the vase body.** Using the flexible pad sander, smooth the join between the vase body ring sets. Feel inside as you sand to be sure you don't remove too much wood.

26 **Gluing the top assembly to the top set of rings.** Place the top assembly on the top set of rings, continuing the spiral. Glue together. Place weight on top and let dry.

27 **Finishing the sanding and shaping.** Using the flexible pad sander, finish shaping and sanding the outside of vase, using progressively finer grits.

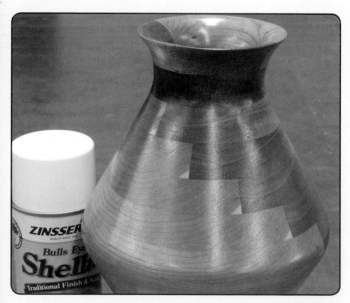

28 **Finishing the vase.** Give the sanded vase several coats of shellac, smoothing between each coat with a 320-grit flexible sanding sponge or 0000 steel wool.

Walnut Vase: A Step-by-Step Guide

Wood

- Redheart, ¾" (1.9cm) thick: center ring 7½" (19.1cm) square
- Veneer, dyed white: 2 each 7½" (19.1cm) square
- Walnut, ¾" (1.9cm) thick: 2 each, top and bottom rings, 7½" (19.1cm) square
- Walnut, ⅛" (3mm) thick: top accent ring, 4" (10.2cm) square

Materials

- Wood glue, Weldbond preferred
- Repositionable adhesive
- Sandpaper
- Shellac
- Spray finish, such as lacquer
- Steel wool: 0000

Tools

- Awl
- Scroll saw blades: #7 blade, Flying Dutchman ultra reverse preferred
- Shop-made angle drilling guides: 30°, 40°
- Drill with bit: #54 wire size or smaller (to fit scroll saw blade)
- Compass
- Bowl press or board and clamps
- Round inflatable sander with sleeves: assorted grit
- Flexible shaft
- Flexible pad sander, 2" (51mm)-dia., with discs: assorted grits
- Belt sander
- Spindle sander or sanding drums, 1½" (38mm), 2" (51mm) dia., with sleeves: assorted grits

While scrollers often make vases by simply inverting one set of rings over another, leaving the interiors unfinished, I had something more ambitious in mind for this project—a gently rounded shape, finished inside and out, and accented with veneered top and center rings. I glued and sanded the vase in several stages, which made it easier to access tight internal spaces and allowed me to use a drill press, instead of a flexible shaft, for most of the interior sanding. If you've mastered simple bowls and are looking for a challenge, this project will move you to the "next level" as you make a vase that any turner would display with pride.

CUTTING THE RINGS

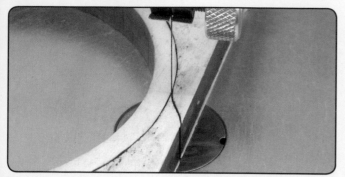

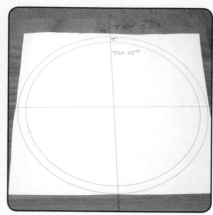

1 **Glue and clamp a piece of veneer to each side of the center ring blank.** Keep the grain of all pieces running in the same direction. Attach the center ring pattern with repositionable adhesive. Drill a blade-entry hole just inside the inner circle. With the saw table level, insert a blade and cut the center. Save the cutout piece for Step 11. Cut the outer circle to complete the center ring. Vacuum thoroughly to prevent migration of the red dust into the pores of the veneer.

2 **Draw intersecting guidelines down the center of the upper and lower ring blanks.** Then, mark the top edges. Attach a copy of the upper and lower rings patterns to each blank with repositionable adhesive, using an awl to match the center of the pattern with the center of the guidelines. Mark the pattern so you can identify the ring sets and the locations of the top edges.

3 **Tilt the left side of the saw table down to 20°.** Starting with the blank for the lower ring set, cut clockwise around the outer ring. Tilt the left side of the saw table down to 30°. Drill a 30° blade-entry hole using a shop-made angle guide. Insert the blade and cut clockwise around the circle to complete the first ring. Remove the pattern and transfer all of the identifying marks to the ring and remainder of the blank.

4 **Place the ring on the remainder of the blank with the tops aligned.** Then, trace the inside of the ring to make the cutting line for the second ring. Drill a blade-entry hole at a 40° angle on this line. Tilt the left side of the saw table down to 40°. Insert the blade and cut clockwise around the circle to complete the second ring. These two rings and the remaining piece form the bottom half of the vase.

5 **Repeat Steps 3 and 4 with the second walnut blank.** This gives you the first two rings for the top half of the vase. Place the second ring on the remainder of the blank and trace the inside. Drill a blade-entry hole at a 40° angle, insert the blade, and cut clockwise around the circle to complete the third ring. The width of the ring on the smaller face should be about ⅝" (1.6cm).

GLUING AND SANDING THE COMPONENTS

6 Position the center ring between the largest rings of the top and bottom sets. Make sure the inner edges match. The center ring should protrude about ⅛" (3mm) on the outside. Glue and clamp the three rings together. (If you're concerned about slippage, you can glue each ring as a separate step.) Let the glue dry. These three glued rings are the beginning of the lower assembly.

7 Tilt the table of a belt or disc sander to 20°. Sand each side of the center ring until it is flush with the adjacent walnut ring. This will make it easier to shape the outside of the vase in Step 17.

8 Sand the inside of the lower assembly. Use a round inflatable sander and an 80-grit sleeve to sand the inside of the assembly until the center ring and surrounding areas of the walnut rings are smooth. Then, switch to a 120-grit sleeve to remove any remaining glue residue and refine the shaping. Avoid sanding near the upper and lower gluing edges. These areas will be sanded when additional rings are added.

9 Glue and clamp the second lower ring to the bottom of the lower assembly. Let the glue dry. Next, glue and clamp the two remaining upper rings. This is the beginning of the upper assembly. Let the glue dry. Set aside the remaining piece from the lower ring set until Step 16.

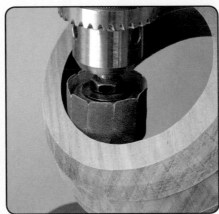

10 Sand the inside of the lower assembly until the surface is smooth and free of glue residue. Sand the inner edge of the second ring to a well-shaped circle. It's easier to do this with the bottom faceup. Set the assembly aside until Step 15.

CHAPTER 6: Thinking Outside the Bowl

COMPLETING THE UPPER ASSEMBLY

11 **Measure the diameter and ring width of the smaller face of the upper assembly.** The diameter should be about 3½" (8.9cm) and the ring width about ⅝" (1.6cm). Use a compass to draw a matching ring on the remainder of the lamination from Step 1. Cut around the outer circle with the saw table level. Glue and clamp the top accent ring blank to the underside with the grain directions aligned. Allow the glue to dry.

12 **Cut away the excess walnut.** Use the outer edge of the redheart ring as a guide. Drill a blade-entry hole inside the inner circle. Insert the saw blade and cut the circle. Sand the outside of the ring until the walnut is flush with the redheart. Sand the inside smooth. Glue and clamp the completed neck, walnut side up, to the upper assembly with the grain directions aligned. Allow the glue to dry.

13 **Sand the joint where the neck meets the angled rings.** Use 1½" (38mm)- and a 2" (51mm)-diameter spindles to sand until the joint is smooth and continuous with no glue residue visible. Use the 2" (51mm) spindle to sand the inside smooth. Try not to remove more wood than necessary to allow more options for shaping in the next step.

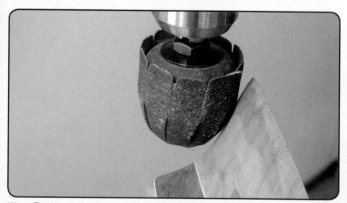

14 **Shape and smooth the inside of the upper assembly.** Use the round inflatable sander with 80- and 120-grit sleeves. Next, shape the outside of the neck and do a preliminary shaping of the outside of the walnut rings. Finally, enlarge the inner diameter of the neck so that the wall is about ¼" (6mm) thick. You will complete the shaping in Step 17, after you have fully assembled the vase.

COMPLETING THE VASE

15 **Glue and clamp the upper and lower assemblies together.** Keep the grain directions aligned and match the inside edges as closely as possible. Let the glue dry.

16 **Sand the inside joints of the two assemblies.** Use 80- and 120-grit sleeves for the round inflatable sander on a flexible shaft. Apply a coat of shellac to the larger face of the bottom piece saved from Step 9 and to the inside of the vase. Do not get shellac on the gluing surfaces. Let the shellac dry. Sand the shellacked surfaces smooth with 320-grit sandpaper and remove all sanding residue. Glue on the bottom piece, keeping the grain directions aligned. To prevent squeeze-out on the top surface of the bottom piece, do not apply glue near the inner edge of the bottom ring. Clamp the vase in a press or between two boards and let the glue dry.

17 **Sand the outside of the vase.** Use a 2" (51mm)-diameter flexible pad sander on the outside of the vase and a round inflatable sander on the neck. Work through the grits up to 220.

18 **Seal the outside of the vase with a coat of shellac.** Smooth the shellac with a 320-grit finishing mop or sandpaper. Apply several coats of lacquer or a finish of your choice, buffing with 0000 steel wool between coats as needed.

CHAPTER 6: Thinking Outside the Bowl

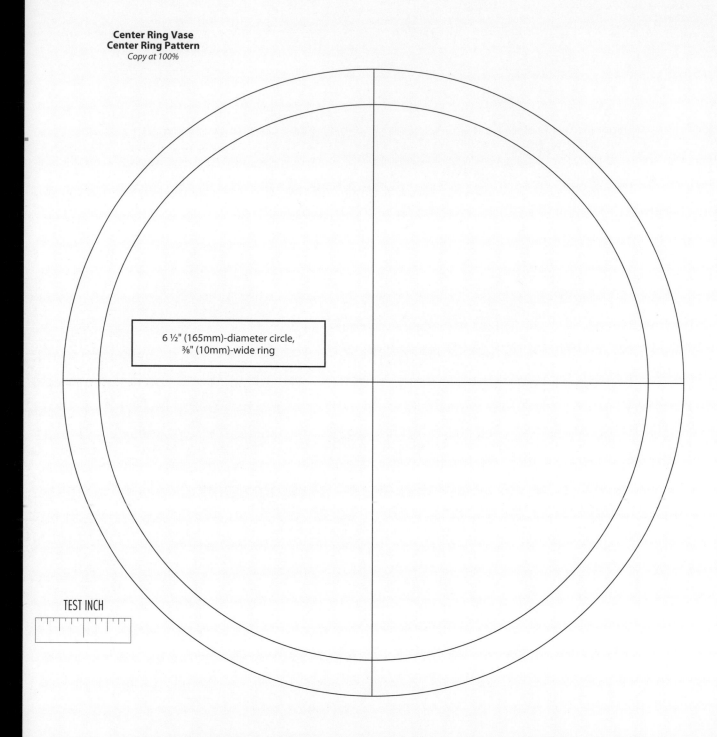

Center Ring Vase
Center Ring Pattern
Copy at 100%

6 ½" (165mm)-diameter circle,
⅜" (10mm)-wide ring

TEST INCH

**Center Ring Vase
Upper and Lower Rings Pattern**
Copy at 100%

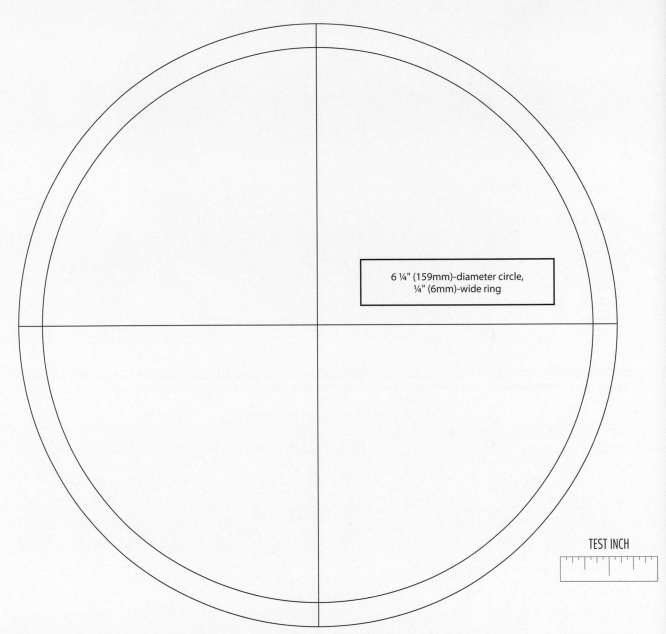

6 ¼" (159mm)-diameter circle,
¼" (6mm)-wide ring

TEST INCH

WALNUT VASE: A STEP-BY-STEP GUIDE

Blooming Petal Bowl: A Step-by-Step Guide

An opening flower is a lovely shape for a bowl. I made this scrolled version from several sets of straight and curved rings, and carved it with sanders to form graceful flaring petals. While this is not my easiest project, the detailed instructions place it well within the reach of anyone with a little bowl-making experience. What makes it exciting is the process of transforming an odd-looking set of rings into an unusual and delicate work of art. While sanding the interior is challenging, working in sections ensures accessibility and results in a bowl that is beautiful both inside and out.

Wood
- Mahogany, ¾" (19mm) thick: 4 each 7" x 7" (179mm x 179mm), preferably cut from a single long board

Materials
- Pencil: white graphite
- Sleeves for large round inflatable sander: assorted
- Sleeves for small round inflatable sander: assorted
- Scalloped discs for pad sander: assorted grits
- Sandpaper
- Steel wool: 0000
- Wood glue, such as Weldbond
- Repositionable adhesive
- Mineral spirits
- Spray shellac
- Spray lacquer

Tools
- Blades: #9 reverse-tooth
- Bowl press or assorted clamps and clamping board
- Awl
- Drill with bit: #54 wire size or ¹⁄₁₆" (2mm) dia.
- Flexible shaft tool
- Shop-made angle guides (see Getting Started, pg.50): 20°, 25°, 35°
- Sanders: large round inflatable, small round inflatable, 2" (51mm)-dia. regular flexible pad sander, 2" (51mm)-dia. soft flexible pad sander
- Spindle sander or sanding drums: ¼" (6mm), ½" (13mm), 1" (25mm) dia.

Getting started

To cut the bowl rings, we will tilt the saw table to a variety of angles. I always tilt the left side of the table down and cut in a clockwise direction. If, for some reason, you can only tilt the right side of your table down, cut in a counterclockwise direction.

To drill angled blade-entry holes, you will need a simple jig and handheld drill. To make the jig, set the saw table to the desired angle and cut a piece of scrap. Hold a drill bit against the angled end of the wood and drill the holes as needed. Drill all of the angled holes toward the center of the blank.

When a project involves multiple blanks, the best way to create the illusion that it has been carved from a single block is to use blanks cut sequentially from the same board. Select one long edge of the board as the top. Place the patterns with the petal marked "top" at that edge and with the horizontal guideline running along the grain. If you are using several pieces of wood, or one wider piece, try to match the grain as closely as possible as you lay out the patterns.

CUTTING THE RINGS

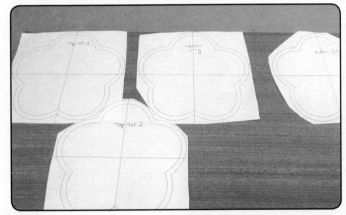

1 **Attach the patterns to the blanks.** Make four copies of the pattern. Mark them as follows: Bottom Rings, Center Ring, First Top Ring, and Flared Top Ring. Using the horizontal guidelines and "top marks" of the patterns for alignment, place the patterns, in sequence, on the wood. Attach them with temporary-bond adhesive. If you have not already done so, cut the wood into individual blanks.

2 **Cut the first bottom ring.** Tilt the saw table 20° and cut around the outer line on the bottom rings blank. Drill a blade-entry hole at a 20° angle on the inner line of the pattern. Insert a saw blade through the hole and cut the inside of the first ring. Remove the pattern, and mark the tops of both the ring and the center remainder of the blank.

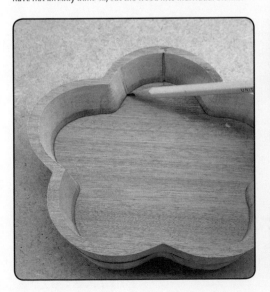

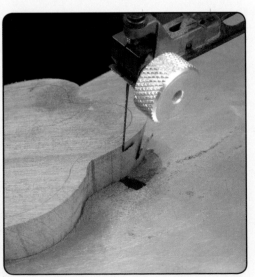

3 **Cut the second bottom ring.** Place the first ring on the remainder of the blank, tops aligned, and trace the inner edge to form the inner cutting line for the second ring. Tilt the saw table to 25°, left side down. Re-cut the perimeter of the blank using the upper edge as a guide. Do not cut into the upper edge. Drill a 25° entry hole on the inner line. Insert the saw blade and cut along the inner line to complete the second ring. Mark the top of the ring and the blank.

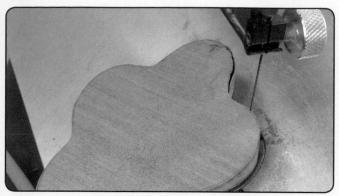

4 **Cut the base.** Place the second ring on the remainder of the wood with the top marks aligned. Trace the outside of the ring to form the cutting line for the base. Tilt the saw table to 35° and cut the base.

5 **Cut the center ring.** Level the saw table, and cut around the outer line of the pattern. Drill a small blade-entry hole on the inner line, as indicated on the pattern. Insert the saw blade and cut around the inner line to complete the ring. Set aside the center piece to use for another project (See page 163).

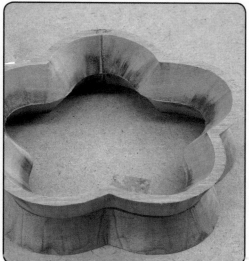

6 **Cut the top rings.** Tilt the saw table to 25°. Using the blank for the first top ring, cut along the outer line. Tilt the saw table to 35°. Drill a blade-entry hole at a 35° angle on the inner line. Insert the saw blade and cut along the inside line to complete the first top ring. This ring will be ¼" (6mm) wide on the larger face and about ½" (13mm) wide on the smaller face. Mark the top. Set aside the center piece to use for another project. Repeat the process to cut a second top ring; flip it over to form the flared ring.

ASSEMBLING THE RINGS

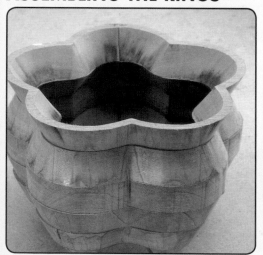

7 **Stack the rings to preview the project.** Transfer the "top" marks to the sides of the rings and base, and remove them from the gluing surfaces. Stack the base and rings to get an overview of the project and to check for spaces between the rings. Sand as needed until the rings lie perfectly flat against each other.

8 **Glue the center assembly.** Glue and clamp the straight center ring to the largest bottom ring and the first top ring, aligning the tops, and allow it to dry.

9 **Sand the center assembly.** Sand the inside of the assembly using a flexible shaft tool with small and large round sanders equipped with coarse and medium-grit sleeves. Use the small sander to access tighter areas and the large sander to smooth and round the inner surface. The goal is to sand a curve into the middle ring and to smooth the glue lines on its upper and lower edges. Be careful not to damage the top and bottom gluing surfaces of the assembly.

10 **Eliminate any glue spots.** Apply mineral spirits to the inside of the assembly. Mark any glue spots that appear with a white pencil and sand them away when the mineral spirits have dried.

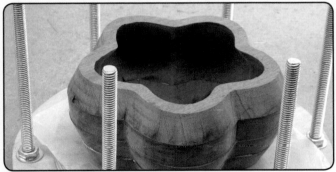

11 **Add the second bottom ring.** Glue and clamp the second bottom ring to the assembly, keeping the tops aligned. Allow it to dry. Then, using the round inflatable sanders, sand the inside until the lower three rings form a smooth continuous curve. Use the small round sander to shape the inside of the bottom edge. Be careful not to damage the gluing surface. Apply mineral spirits and sand away any glue spots.

SHAPING THE PROJECT

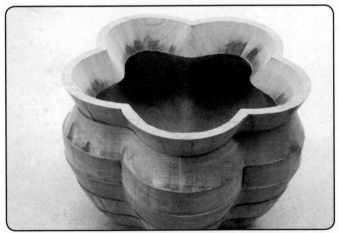

12 **Attach the remaining rings.** Glue and clamp the base to the assembly, keeping the tops aligned. Allow it to dry for five minutes, remove the clamps, and clean up any glue squeeze-out. Then, glue on the flared top ring, keeping the tops aligned. Reclamp the assembly and let the glue dry.

13 **Sand the inside of the flared ring.** Use the large round sander and the coarse sleeve to sand the inside of the flared ring to remove burn and blade marks, to soften the joint between the two top rings, and to sand down the pointed pieces of wood between the petals until they are about ¼" (6mm) thick.

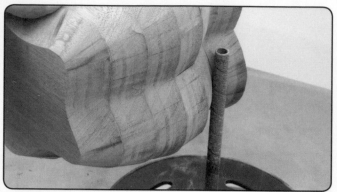

14 **Sand the joint between the top rings.** Use a ¼" (6mm)-diameter spindle or drum sander to sand the accessible parts of the outside of the joint between the top rings. If you are using a spindle sander, rotate and lift the bowl for maximum access. Sand until the glued edges of the top rings form a continuous curve. The curve will be enlarged and the inaccessible area will be removed when you shape the petals in later steps.

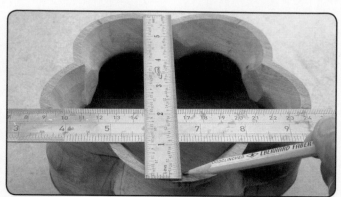

15 **Mark the center of each petal.** The top of each petal is about 3" (76mm) at its widest. Use two rulers and the opposite point to mark the center of each petal. Starting at that mark, draw a short vertical line down the outside of the petal. This line will help keep you oriented as you shape each petal in later steps.

SHAPING THE PROJECT

16 **Sand the outside of the bowl.** Use a 2" (51mm)-diameter pad sander and an 80-grit disc with scalloped edges to remove ridges and burn and blade marks from the outside of the bowl. Work from the bottom of the bowl up to the center ring, and from the first top ring down to the center ring. Do not sand the flared ring or the areas where the top two rings meet. Repeat with a 120-grit scalloped disc to remove any scratch marks and refine the shape.

17 **Sand through the center of the space between the petals.** Use a 1" (25mm)-diameter spindle sander to sand along the inside points between the petals until a hole appears. Each hole should be centered between a pair of petals.

18 **Start shaping the top edge.** Continue sanding between the petals, angling the bowl back and forth until you create a curve at the top of the space between each pair of petals.

19 **Increase the spaces between the petals.** Start at the curve sanded into the top edge and use the 1" (25mm) spindle to deepen the space between each pair of petals. Sand to just below the glue line for the flared top ring.

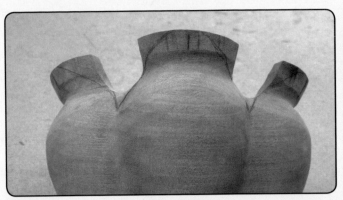

20 Draw a shaping guide for the upper edge. Darken the lines drawn in Step 15. Use a pencil to draw a rough guide for the top shaping of each petal. The lowest point between the petals should be at the next glue line. Be conservative with the shaping at this point because you will remove more wood later.

21 Refine the shape. Working from the top edge down, and staying centered between the petals, use the large round sander with the coarse sleeve to roughly define the shape of each petal and to remove excess wood from the areas between the petals. Switch to the small round sander and the coarse sleeve when the large sander becomes too large to use.

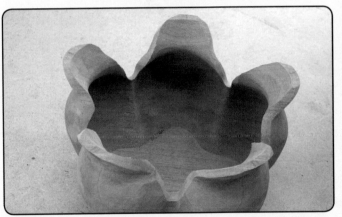

22 Continue shaping the petals. Use a ¼" (6mm) spindle or drum sander to extend the space between the petals to the top of the straight ring and to shape the sides of the petals.

23 Shape the undersides of the petals. Use a ¼" (6mm) to ½" (13mm)-diameter spindle or drum sander to begin shaping the underside of each petal. Switch to the small round sander with a coarse sleeve to smooth the curves.

24 Shape the inside of each petal. Use the large round sander with the coarse sleeve to thin the inside of each petal from the bottom to the tip and to thin the top edge of the incurving area between the petals. Check wood thickness frequently to avoid sanding away too much. After the final sanding in Step 28, the walls should be about ⅛" (3mm) thick.

Protecting the sanding sleeve

The openings in the bottom part of the sleeves of the large round sander tend to catch on edges and tear. To prevent this, use the upper section of the sleeve near the edges, or switch to the small round sander whose sleeves are less likely to catch and tear.

CHAPTER 6: Thinking Outside the Bowl

BLOOMING PETAL BOWL: A STEP-BY-STEP GUIDE

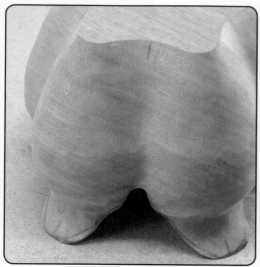

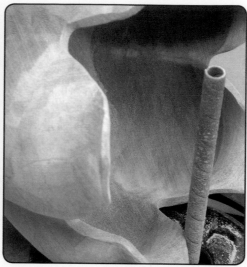

25 Finish contouring the petals. Re-draw the midpoint of each petal. Use a pencil to draw the final contour of each petal. With the large round sander, thin any thick edges that become visible as you shape the sides of the petal. Use the small round sander and the ¼" (6mm) spindle to access the smaller areas and complete the shaping. Finish with the large round sander to remove excess wood from the inside of the petals so that all edges are the same thickness.

26 Contour the bottom of the bowl. Use the large round sander to accentuate the spaces between petals on the bottom edge of the bowl.

COMPLETING THE PROJECT

27 Sand the bowl. Sand the exterior and interior of the bowl, using the round and pad sanders to remove irregularities and bumps and to sand all edges to the same thickness—about ⅛" (3mm). Sand through the grits, using medium and fine-grit sleeves for the round sanders and working up to 220-grit with the pad sander.

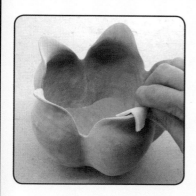

28 Finish sanding the bowl. Hand-sand the edges with 220-grit sandpaper until they are smooth and even. Feel the surface of the bowl carefully and sand away any small ridges or bumps. If irregularities are too large to remove by hand, use the pad or round sanders to remove them and then finish the sanding by hand. Then, use a pad sander with a soft foam pad to sand the outside of the bowl to 320-grit. The soft pad prevents distortion of the established shape.

29 Finish the bowl. Apply mineral spirits to the outside of the bowl to check for glue spots; sand away any that appear. Seal the bowl with spray shellac, and sand it smooth with 320-grit sandpaper. Remove any sanding dust with a tack cloth, and then apply several coats of clear spray lacquer.

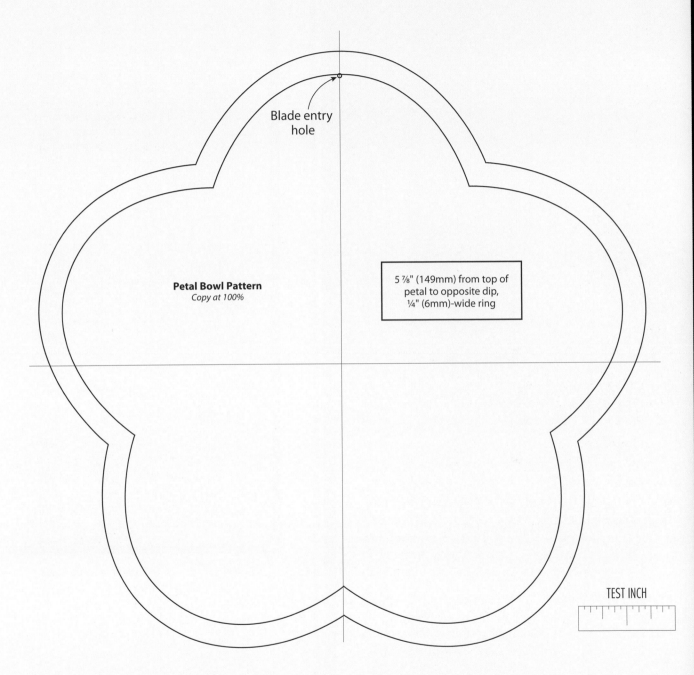

Blade entry
hole

Petal Bowl Pattern
Copy at 100%

5 ⅞" (149mm) from top of
petal to opposite dip,
¼" (6mm)-wide ring

TEST INCH

BLOOMING PETAL BOWL: A STEP-BY-STEP GUIDE

Ginger Jar

Wood

JAR:
- (3) 7" x 7" x ¾" (178mm x 178mm x 19mm) maple

LID:
- (1) 4" x 4" x ¼" (102mm x 102mm x 6mm) maple

BASE:
- (1) 5½" x 5½" x ¾" (140mm x 140mm x 19mm) teak

BASE RING:
- (1) 4½" x 4½" x ¼" (114mm x 114mm x 6mm) teak

Materials
- Packing tape (optional)
- Glue
- Repositionable adhesive
- Sanding discs for flexible pad sander, assorted grits 60 to 400
- Sandpaper for inflatable ball sander, assorted grits 60 to 320 (optional)
- Sandpaper for hand sanding, assorted grits 220 to 400
- 0000 steel wool or 320-grit sanding sponge
- Spray shellac or Danish oil
- Rubber band for clamping base
- Blue tape for masking base

Tools
- Scroll saw blade, size #9
- Drill bit size #54 or 1/16" (2mm)
- Awl
- Ruler
- Bowl press or clamps
- 2" (51mm) flexible pad sander
- Inflatable ball sander and pump (optional)

A ceramic ginger jar lamp on a brass base served as the model for this project. The jar itself was not difficult to replicate—it's simply a small curved bowl inverted on a straight one with a straight ring between—but the cutout sides of the base posed a challenge. The solution was simple once I realized that by using a single square of wood, cut diagonally into four pieces and trimmed, I could make compound cuts on the sides to create the pattern I wanted.

When making the jar, it's important to keep the grain of the different ring sets running in the same direction. This helps create the illusion that the jar is cut from a single piece of wood. I chose teak for the base, but another dark wood, like walnut, could be used.

MAKING RING SET 1

1. For the first set of rings, which forms the bottom part of the jar, draw guidelines on one of the 7" (178mm) pieces of maple and glue on the pattern for ring set 1 (page 166) with repositionable adhesive.

2. With the scroll saw table tilted 20°, left side down, cut clockwise along the outer circle. Drill a 20° entry hole on the inner circle and make the cut to complete the first ring.

3. Place the first ring on the blank. Transfer the guidelines, mark the top, and trace the outline of the second ring. Drill a 20° entry hole and cut out the second ring. Use the second ring to mark the third ring.

MAKING THE CENTER RING

1. For the center ring, which will go between the top and the bottom ring sets of the jar, glue the pattern for the center ring (page 166) to a second piece of 7" (178mm) maple with repositionable adhesive.

2. Cut along the outer circle with the saw table level.

MAKING RING SET 2

1. For the second set of rings, which will become the top of the jar, draw guidelines on the third 7" (178mm) piece of maple.

2. Glue on the pattern for ring set 2 (page 166) with repositionable adhesive.

3. Cut along the outer circle with the saw table set at 34°, left side down, cutting clockwise.

4. Cut out the third ring. You now have three rings—each ¼" (6mm) wide—and a base.

5. Glue up the rings, clamp, and let dry.

6. Sand the inside lightly with a flexible pad or inflatable ball sander to smooth any ridges. Keep the sides as thick as possible to allow for shaping of the outside of the jar.

7. Glue on the base, clamp, and let dry.

3. Drill a straight entry hole just inside the inner ring and cut out the ring. You will have a straight-sided single ring, ½" (13mm) wide. Reserve the center piece that is left for making the top lip and lid.

4. Drill a 34° entry hole on the inner circle and complete the ring. You will have one ½" (13mm)-wide ring and a base.

5. Glue the ring to the base, clamp, and let dry.

6. Sand the inside lightly. Invert so that the bottom side is up. This will be the top of the jar.

MAKING THE LIP AND LID

1. Glue lid pattern (page 168) with repositionable adhesive to the piece saved from the center ring.

2. Drill a straight entry hole just inside the innermost ring and cut out the center with the saw table level. This center piece will not be used for this project.

3. Drill a straight entry hole on the next circle and cut along the line to complete the lip of the jar.

4. Sand the lip smooth. This is the part of the jar that the lid will fit over.

5. Sand the sides of the circle left in the remaining piece. Glue this piece to the ¼" (6mm)-thick piece of maple. Keep the grain of both pieces running in the same direction. Clamp and let dry.

6. Cut along the outer ring. This piece is the lid. When inverted, it will fit nicely over the lip.

7. Sand to soften the top and bottom edges of the lid, and the top edge of the lip.

5 Making the lip and lid. The lid, shown next to the lip, is ready for cutting.

ASSEMBLING THE JAR

1. Center the lip on the top of the jar (inverted ring set 2), aligning the grain, and trace the inside. This should be about a 2" (51mm) circle.

2. Drill a straight entry hole just inside the circle. With the saw table level, cut out the circle.

3. Glue the lip in place, keeping the grains aligned. Weight down and let dry.

4. Sand the inside of the lip flush with the inside of the jar.

5. Glue the center ring to ring set 2 (top of the jar), keeping grains aligned. Clamp and let dry.

6. Glue this assembly to ring set 1 (bottom of jar), keeping grains aligned. Weight down and let dry.

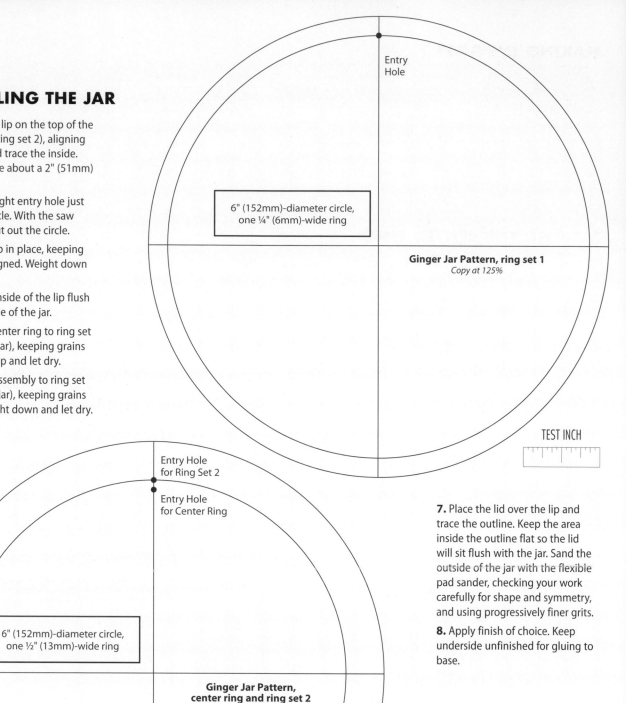

Entry Hole

6" (152mm)-diameter circle, one ¼" (6mm)-wide ring

Ginger Jar Pattern, ring set 1
Copy at 125%

TEST INCH

Entry Hole for Ring Set 2

Entry Hole for Center Ring

6" (152mm)-diameter circle, one ½" (13mm)-wide ring

**Ginger Jar Pattern,
center ring and ring set 2**
Copy at 125%
(Make two copies)

TEST INCH

7. Place the lid over the lip and trace the outline. Keep the area inside the outline flat so the lid will sit flush with the jar. Sand the outside of the jar with the flexible pad sander, checking your work carefully for shape and symmetry, and using progressively finer grits.

8. Apply finish of choice. Keep underside unfinished for gluing to base.

MAKING THE BASE

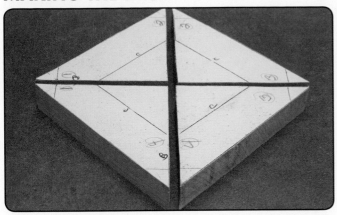

1 Cutting the outline and diagonals. You will need two copies of the top pattern (page 169) and four of the side pattern (page 169). Glue the base top pattern to the 5½" (140mm) piece of teak with repositionable adhesive and cut along the outline (A). Cut along the diagonals (B) to form four pieces. Mark the pieces as shown so you can reassemble them properly later.

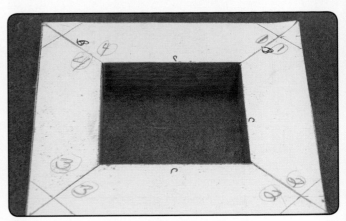

2 Cutting the inner lines. Cut along the inner lines (C).

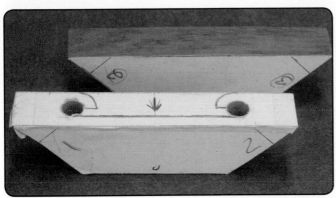

3 Laying out the sides. Glue a copy of the base side pattern (page 169, top) or the alternate base side pattern (page 169, bottom) with repositionable adhesive to the outside face of each piece. Drill two 3/8" (10mm) holes where indicated.

4 Cutting the sides. Cut along the pattern lines. Use supports if desired.

5 Gluing the base. Remove the patterns. Glue the four pieces together. Clamp with a rubber band and let dry.

6 Shaping the base. Use the base top pattern as a guide for cutting off the four corners. Round the corners and soften the top edges.

7 **Cutting the beveled circle.** Place the ginger jar on the 4½" (114mm) piece of teak and trace the lower profile. Tilt the saw table 20°, left side down, and cut along the line counterclockwise. This will give you an outward flaring circle with a top diameter that matches the bottom of the jar. Glue the circle to the top of the base. Weight down and let dry. Sand smooth.

8 **Finishing the base.** Cover the face of the circle with blue tape, leaving a small outer edge uncovered. Apply finish of choice to base. Remove the tape. Glue the ginger jar to the base, weight down, and let dry.

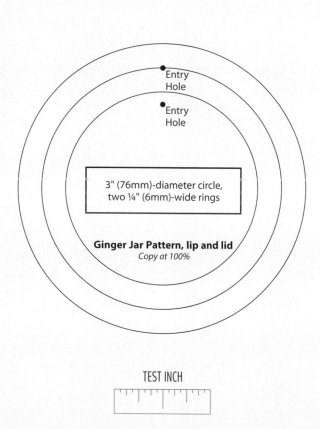

Entry
Hole

Entry
Hole

3" (76mm)-diameter circle,
two ¼" (6mm)-wide rings

Ginger Jar Pattern, lip and lid
Copy at 100%

TEST INCH

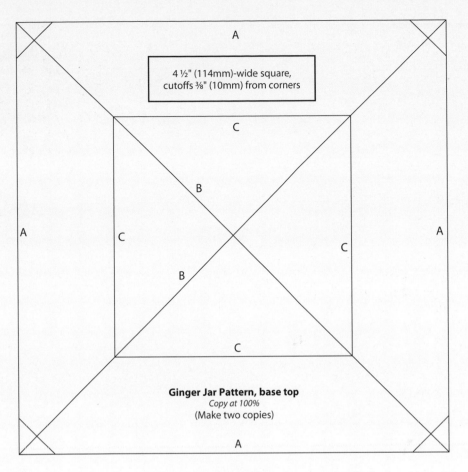

A

4 ½" (114mm)-wide square,
cutoffs ⅜" (10mm) from corners

C

B

A   A

C

C

C

B

C

Ginger Jar Pattern, base top
Copy at 100%
(Make two copies)

A

TEST INCH

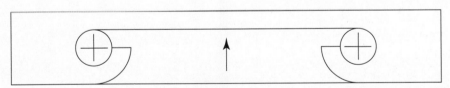

Ginger Jar Pattern, base sides
Copy at 100%
(Make four copies)

4 ½" L x ¾" W (114mm L x 19mm W)
rectangle, both bases

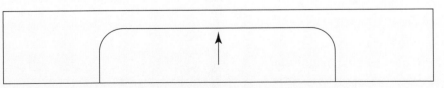

Ginger Jar Pattern, alternate base sides
Copy at 100%
(Make two copies)

GINGER JAR

Footed Candy Dish

At a juried crafts show I attended, the large number of lathe-turned bowls that combined bloodwood and cherry to good effect impressed me. This project uses that combination to create an easy-to-make footed candy dish with a scalloped edge. Both cherry and bloodwood are dense and tend to burn, but if you use tape and change blades frequently, you should not have a problem. Also, the rings are generous in width and any burn marks can easily be sanded away.

The initial appearance of the scallops is somewhat alarming: while those on the outside take shape immediately, those on the inside won't look right until you contour the inside of the rim.

Because of the steep angle of the first ring, the outer edge of the second ring must be recut to avoid the need for excessive sanding.

Wood

DISH:

- (1) 7" x 7" x ¾" (178mm x 178mm x 19mm) cherry
- (4) 3" x ½" x ¾" (76mm x 13mm x 19mm) bloodwood
- (4) 5" x ½" x ¾" (127mm x 13mm x 19mm) bloodwood

PEDESTAL BASE:

- (1) 4" x 4" x ¾" (102mm x 102mm x 19mm) cherry
- (1) 3" x 3" x ¾" (76mm x 76mm x 19mm) cherry

Materials

- Packing tape
- Glue
- Repositionable adhesive
- Sanding discs for flexible pad sander, assorted grits 60 to 400
- Sandpaper for inflatable ball sander, assorted grits 60 to 320 (optional)
- Sandpaper for hand sanding, assorted grits 220 to 400
- 0000 steel wool or 320-grit sanding sponge
- Spray shellac or Danish oil

Tools

- Scroll saw blade, size #9
- Drill bit size #54 or 1/16" (2mm)
- Awl
- Ruler
- Compass
- Bowl press or clamps
- Clamps for lamination
- 2" (51mm) flexible pad sander
- Inflatable ball sander and pump (optional)

LAMINATION GUIDE

1. Glue the lamination pattern and guide (below) to the 7" (178mm) piece of cherry with repositionable adhesive and cut out the perimeter.

2. Mark the center of the blank with a small awl mark.

3. Sand the edges smooth.

4. Refer to the lamination pattern and guide (below) to apply the bloodwood border. Glue two 3" pieces of bloodwood to opposite sides of the octagon (A). Clamp and let dry.

5. Glue two 3" (76mm) pieces of bloodwood to the set of opposite sides (B). Clamp and let dry.

6. Trim the bloodwood so the edges are flush with the unglued sides. You now have two sets of opposite sides that do not yet have bloodwood glued to them—C and D.

7. Glue two 5" (127mm) pieces of bloodwood to the set of opposite sides (C). Clamp and let dry.

8. Glue the last two 5" (127mm) pieces to the remaining set of sides (D). Clamp and let dry.

9. Trim the bloodwood so the edges are flush.

10. Sand both faces of the blank smooth.

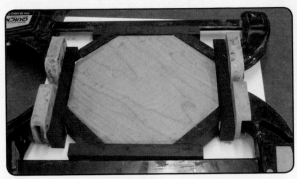

8 Gluing. Glue and clamp the last set of bloodwood strips to the cherry blank.

9 Trimming. Trim the edges of the bloodwood.

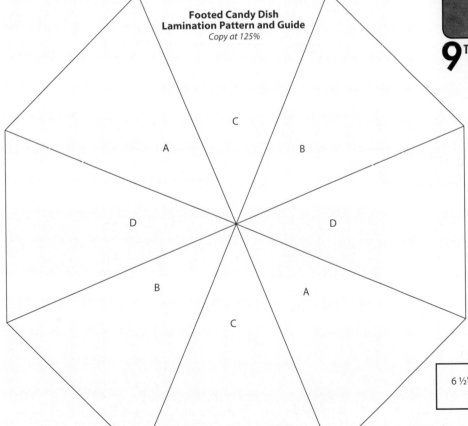

**Footed Candy Dish
Lamination Pattern and Guide**
Copy at 125%

C

A   B

D   D

B   A

C

TEST INCH

6 ½" (165mm)-wide octagon
lamination pattern

FOOTED CANDY DISH

MAKING THE DISH

1. Mark guidelines on the blank.

2. Using the center mark and an awl, glue the cutting pattern (opposite) to the bowl blank with repositionable adhesive, aligning guidelines.

3. Cut the perimeter clockwise at a 40° angle with the saw table tilted left side down.

4. Drill a 40° entry hole and cut along the inner circle to complete the first ring.

5. Place the ring on the bowl blank, align the guidelines, and mark both sides of the ring to create the cutting lines for the second ring.

6. Cut clockwise along the outer edge of the second ring with the table tilted 38°, left side down. This cut removes the excess material that remains when a ring is cut at an angle that is much steeper than usual.

7. Drill a 38° entry hole and cut the inner edge of the second ring at a 38° angle.

8. Place the second ring on the blank, align the guidelines, and draw just the outer perimeter to form the outline for the bottom piece.

9. Cut out the bottom piece at a 45° angle, saw table left side down, cutting clockwise. This is the piece to which you will attach the pedestal base.

10. Glue up the two rings. Clamp and let dry.

11. Sand the inside smooth. Be sure to keep the lower edge round. Contour the upper edge to bring out the scallop effect. The more you sand, the more pronounced the scallops become.

12. Glue on the bottom piece. Clamp and let dry.

13. Sand the outside smooth, contouring the lower edge.

MAKING THE PEDESTAL BASE

1. Using a compass, draw a 3" (76mm) circle on the 4" (102mm) piece of cherry.

2. Cut clockwise along on the circle at a 28° angle, saw table tilted left side down.

3. Trace the outline of the smaller face of the piece you just cut on the 3" (76mm) piece of cherry.

4. With the saw table level, cut out the circle. This piece will form the neck of the pedestal base.

5. Glue both pieces together, keeping the grains aligned. Clamp and let dry.

6. Contour the pedestal using a spindle sander.

7. Glue the pedestal to the bowl. Weight down and let dry.

8. Do touch-up sanding as needed and finish as desired.

5 **Neck and base.** Glue the neck and base together.

7 **Attaching the pedestal.** Glue the pedestal to the bowl.

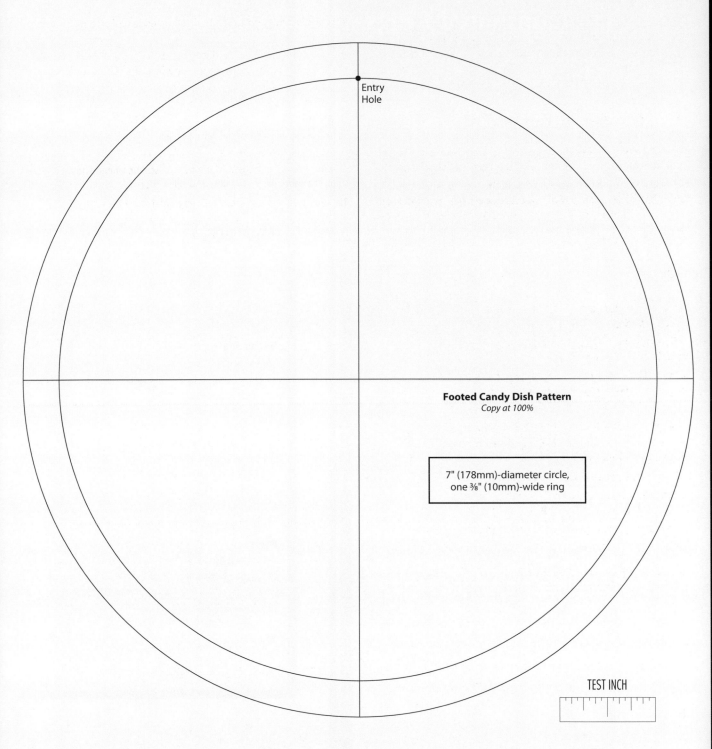

Entry
Hole

Footed Candy Dish Pattern
Copy at 100%

7" (178mm)-diameter circle,
one ⅜" (10mm)-wide ring

TEST INCH

FOOTED CANDY DISH

Rounded Vase with Laminated Rings

This colorful vase uses a two-step cutting process to create contour, and inserts of contrasting wood to add color and interest. While many steps are required, the construction is quite simple: two bowls joined with a center ring, topped by a matching neck assembly. The vase uses a lamination for the center ring, but a solid ring will also work, and is given as an option. Be sure to keep the grain running in the same direction for all pieces.

Wood

BODY OF VASE:
- (2) 7½" x 7½" x ¾" (191mm x 191mm x 19mm) mahogany
- (2) 6" x 6" x 1/8" (152mm x 152mm x 3mm) purpleheart

CENTER RING:
- (1) 7" (178mm) round completed lamination from the Eight-Segment Bowl, page 114
- (2) 7½" x 7½" x 1/8" (191mm x 191mm x 3mm) purpleheart

ALTERNATE CENTER RING:
- (1) 7½" x 7½" x ½" (191mm x 191mm x 13mm) purpleheart

NECK OF VASE:
- (1) 4" x 4" x ¾" (102mm x 102mm x 19mm) mahogany

TOP RIM OF VASE:
- (1) 5" x 5" x ¾" (127mm x 127mm x 19mm) mahogany

Materials
- Packing tape (optional)
- Glue
- Repositionable adhesive
- Sanding discs for flexible pad sander, assorted grits 60 to 400
- Sandpaper for inflatable ball sander, assorted grits 60 to 320
- Sandpaper for hand sanding, assorted grits 220 to 400
- 0000 steel wool or 320-grit sanding sponge
- Spray shellac or Danish oil

Tools
- Scroll saw blade, size #9
- Drill bit size #54 or 1/16" (2mm)
- Awl
- Ruler
- Compass
- Bowl press or clamps
- 2" (51mm) flexible pad sander
- Inflatable ball sander and pump

MAKING THE LOWER SECTION OF THE VASE BODY

1. Draw guidelines on one 7½" (191mm) mahogany blank and glue the vase body pattern (page 177) in place with repositionable adhesive, using the awl to align it with the guidelines.

2. Cut the outline of the first ring at a 20° angle, saw table tilted left side down, cutting clockwise.

3. Drill a 20° entry hole and complete the first ring.

4. Mark the top of the first ring and transfer the guidelines.

5. Place the first ring on the blank and mark the outline for the second ring.

6. Drill a 25° entry hole for the second ring.

7. Before cutting out the second ring, re-cut the outside of the blank at 25°, keeping the top edge the same size. This extra cut adds contour and reduces the amount of shaping needed when you sand the vase.

8. Cut the inside of the second ring at 25°.

9. Place the second ring, narrow side down, on one of the 6" (152mm) pieces of 1/8" (3mm) purpleheart and trace the inner and outer outlines. Keep the grains oriented in the same direction.

10. Drill a 25° entry hole on the inner circle of the purpleheart.

11. Cut clockwise along both circles at a 25° angle to form the third ring. Save the center piece of purpleheart to use for the neck lamination.

12. Place the purpleheart ring on the mahogany blank and use it to mark the inner and outer outlines of the fourth ring.

13. Drill a 30° entry hole on the inner ring and cut the fourth ring at 30°, saw table tilted left side down, cutting clockwise.

14. Trace only the outer perimeter of the fourth ring on the remainder of the mahogany blank.

15. Cut along the traced line at 35°, saw table left side down, cutting clockwise. This piece will be the bottom of the vase.

MAKING THE UPPER SECTION OF THE VASE BODY

1. Repeat Steps 1–12 of "Making the lower section of the vase body."

2. Drill a 35° entry hole on the inner circle of the fourth ring and cut the fourth ring at 35°, saw table tilted left side down, cutting clockwise. The remaining piece of the blank will be the bottom of the neck assembly. It is left as-is to allow maximum wood for shaping in Step 3 of "Completing the vase."

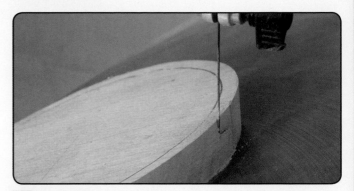

7 **Trimming the second ring.** Trim the outside of the second ring at 25°, but do not cut the top edge.

9 **Trace the outlines of the second ring onto the purpleheart.** Note the piece shown is round because it was a remainder from another project.

ASSEMBLING THE LOWER AND UPPER SECTION

1. Glue up the four rings (three mahogany and one purpleheart) for each section of the vase. Clamp and let dry.

2. Sand the inside of each ring set lightly, since it will not be seen.

3. Glue the vase bottom to the lower ring set. Clamp and let dry.

4. Sand the outside of both parts of the vase body to remove ridges. Final shaping and sanding will be done when the vase is assembled.

Another use for inserted rings

Although contrasting rings are usually inserted for decorative purposes, you can use them to replace rings that have been miscut or damaged. If you can incorporate the substitution into your design, no one will know you didn't plan it that way.

MAKING THE LOWER SECTION OF THE VASE BODY

1A. If using the laminated blank from the Eight Segment Bowl, glue the two 7½" x 7½" x 1/8" (191mm x 191mm x 3mm) pieces of purpleheart to the lamination, one on each face. Keep the grains of the purpleheart aligned. Clamp and let dry. Mark center. Attach the center ring pattern (page 177) with repositionable adhesive and cut a straight-sided ring 6½" (165mm) in diameter and 3/8" (10mm) wide. Save the piece left over to use in another project.

1B. If you're using a ½" (13mm) piece of purpleheart for the center of the vase, use the center ring pattern (page 177) to cut a straight-sided ring 6½" (165mm) in diameter and 3/8" (10mm) wide. Save the piece left over for another project.

2. Glue the decorative ring to the lower section of the vase. Clamp and let dry.

MAKING THE NECK ASSEMBLY

1. Measure the diameter of the larger face of the piece reserved from the top ring set. This piece is the bottom of the neck assembly. It should be about 4¼" (108mm).

2. Draw a circle of the measured diameter on the 5" x 5" x ¾" (127mm x 127mm x 19mm) piece of mahogany. Do not trace the bottom of the neck assembly—if the piece is irregular, the error will be compounded. If a true circle is cut, any irregularities can be more easily corrected.

3. Cut out the circle clockwise at a 35° angle, saw table tilted left side down. This piece is the top of the neck assembly.

4. Glue the 4" x 4" x ¾" (102mm x 102mm x 19mm) piece of mahogany between the two pieces of 1/8" (3mm) purpleheart that were left over after cutting the purpleheart rings for the body of the vase. Keep the grains running in the same direction. This will be the middle of the neck assembly. Clamp and let dry.

5. Place the top piece of the neck assembly, wide side up, on the middle piece and trace the lower edge to form a circle. Mark the center of this circle.

6. Use a compass to draw a circle inside the one you just drew that will give you a ring that is about ½" (13mm) wide. You need a wide ring to allow for shaping in Step 12.

7. With the saw table level, cut along both circles, drilling an entry hole to cut out the middle. This is the completed middle piece of the neck assembly.

8. Place the top piece of the neck assembly so that the larger face is down. Center the completed middle piece on top and trace the inner circle. Repeat for the bottom piece of the neck assembly. See photo for Double Swirl Vase, Step 19, page 147.

9. For both top and bottom pieces of the neck assembly, drill a 35° angle entry hole on the circle drawn in Step 8. The hole should face the edge, not the center.

10. Cut out the center hole for both pieces with the table tilted at 35°, left side down, cutting counterclockwise. Discard the center cut-out piece. See photo for Double Swirl Vase, Step 20, page 147.

11. Glue the middle of the neck assembly between the upper and lower pieces, keeping the grains aligned. See photo for Double Swirl Vase, Step 22, page 147. Clamp and let dry.

12. Shape the neck assembly on the spindle sander and smooth the center hole. Use the inflatable ball sander to contour the upper rim. See photos for Double Swirl Vase, Steps 23 and 24, pages 147–148.

COMPLETING THE VASE

1. Glue the upper part of the vase body to the lower part, keeping the grains aligned. Weight down and let dry.

2. Glue the neck assembly on top, keeping grains aligned. Place weight on top and let dry.

3. Complete the shaping and sanding.

4. Finish as desired.

1 **The three assemblies prior to gluing.** The neck center hole has not been cut yet in this photo.

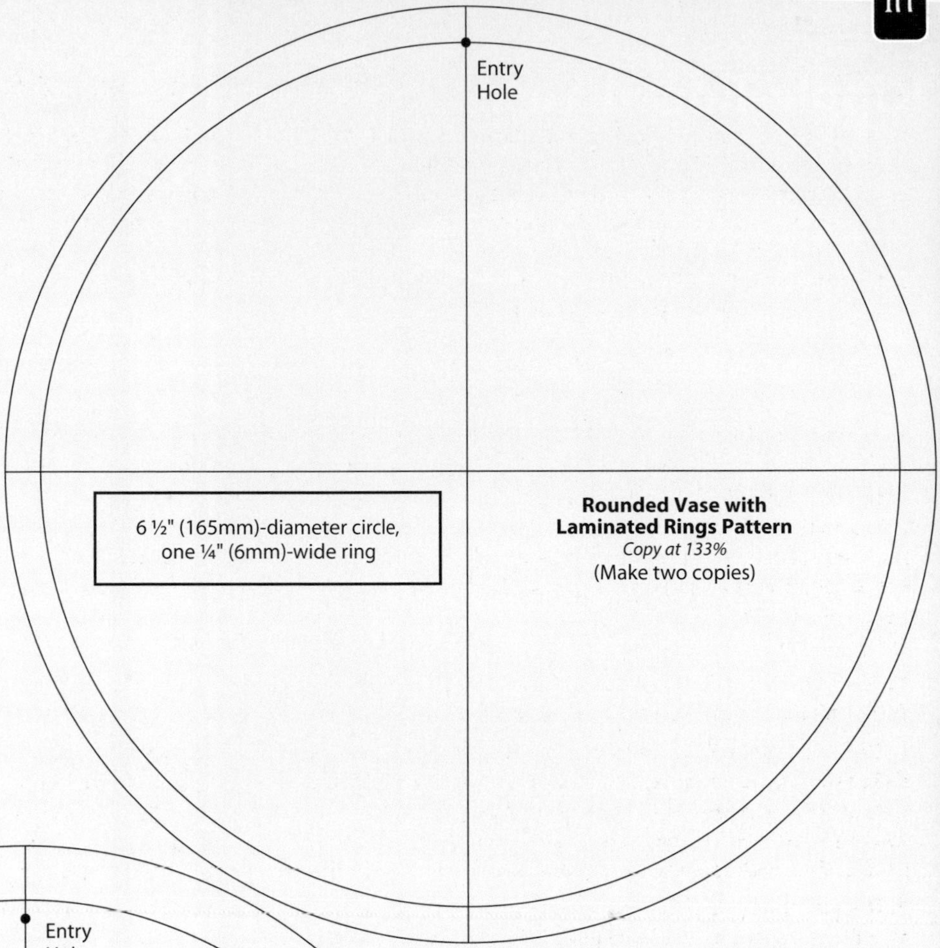

Entry Hole

TEST INCH

6 ½" (165mm)-diameter circle, one ¼" (6mm)-wide ring

Rounded Vase with Laminated Rings Pattern
Copy at 133%
(Make two copies)

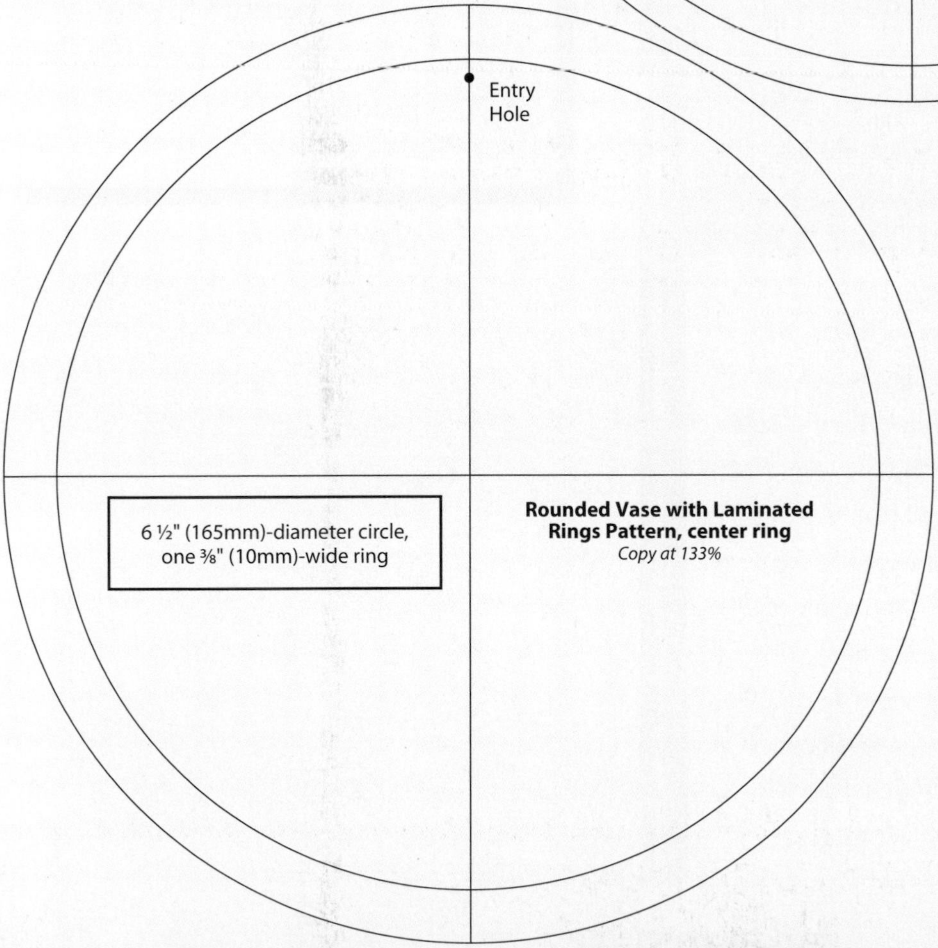

Entry Hole

6 ½" (165mm)-diameter circle, one ⅜" (10mm)-wide ring

Rounded Vase with Laminated Rings Pattern, center ring
Copy at 133%

TEST INCH

Ripple-Edged Vase

Wood

RING SETS 1, 2, AND 3:
- (3) 6" x 6" x ¾" (152mm x 152mm x 19mm) aspen

TOP RING:
- (1) 5" x 5" x ¾" (127mm x 127mm x 19mm) aspen

NECK RING:
- (1) 4" x 4" x ¾" (102mm x 102mm x 19mm) aspen

Materials
- Packing tape (optional)
- Glue
- Repositionable adhesive
- Sanding discs for flexible pad sander, assorted grits 60 to 400
- Sandpaper for inflatable ball sander, assorted grits 60 to 320
- Sandpaper for hand sanding, assorted grits 220 to 400
- 0000 steel wool or 320-grit sanding sponge
- Spray shellac

Tools
- Scroll saw blade, size #9
- Drill bit size #54 or 1/16" (2mm)
- Awl
- Ruler
- Bowl press or clamps
- 2" (51mm) flexible pad sander
- Inflatable ball sander and pump

This elegant vase is the wooden version of a glass one that came with a bouquet of Mother's Day flowers. It uses the same top rim as the Ripple-Edged Round Bowl, page 101, but in a smaller version. As with the other projects in this chapter, it is constructed from several sets of rings. I decided to use aspen for its ivory-like appearance, which I felt complemented the shape of the vase. I also liked the idea of ending the book with a complex project made from the same wood as the very first simple bowl, to highlight the versatility of the techniques underlying the construction of scroll saw bowls.

Note: The vase is constructed in three sections: body, neck, and top ring, each completed before being joined together. The only component that may cause difficulty is the top ring, whose small size makes sanding quite demanding. However, because this piece uses very little wood, you can make more than one, if necessary, until you are satisfied with the results. As always, when using several different pieces of wood, it is important to keep the grain running in the same direction.

MAKING THE BODY

1. Draw guidelines on one of the 6" (152mm) pieces of aspen and glue on the pattern for ring set 1 (page 182) with repositionable adhesive.

2. Cut along the outer line at a 20° angle, saw table tilted left side down, cutting clockwise.

3. Drill a 20° entry hole and complete the first ring.

4. Place the first ring on the bowl blank, mark the top, and transfer guidelines. Mark the outline for the second ring.

5. Drill a 20° entry hole.

6. Cut out and mark the second ring.

7. Cut out and mark the third ring in the same manner.

8. Glue up the three rings, clamp, and let dry.

9. Sand inside lightly, since it will not be seen.

10. Glue on the bottom piece. Clamp and let dry. Sand the outside smooth, keeping the top edge as wide as possible.

11. Glue the pattern for the center ring (page 182) to a second 6" (152mm) piece of aspen with repositionable adhesive.

12. With the saw table level, cut along the outer circle.

13. Drill a straight entry hole just inside the inner ring and cut out the ring. Save the center piece to use for one of the neck rings.

14. Draw guidelines on the third 6" (152mm) piece of aspen and glue on the pattern for ring set 2 (page 182) with repositionable adhesive.

15. Cut along the outer circle with the saw table set at 34°, left side down, cutting clockwise.

16. Drill a 34° entry hole on the inner circle and complete the ring, cutting clockwise. You will have one ring and a remaining piece.

17. Tilt the saw table to 45°, left side down. Using the top edge as a guide, cut clockwise around the perimeter of the remaining piece, wider side up. The top edge should remain the same size.

18. Glue this piece to the ring. Clamp and let dry.

19. Sand inside lightly.

8 Glue up the three rings of set 1.

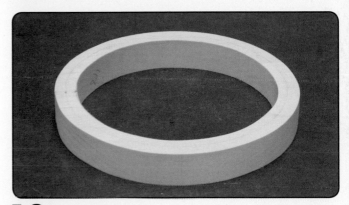

13 Cut out center ring.

18 Glue-up ring set 2.

MAKING THE RIPPLED TOP RING

1. Glue the pattern for the top ring (page 183) to the 5" (127mm) piece of aspen with repositionable adhesive.

2. Cut along the outer circle of the ring at a 35° angle, saw table tilted left side down, cutting clockwise.

3. Drill a 25° entry hole just inside the inner circle and cut along the inner circle at a 25° angle, saw table left side down, cutting clockwise. The bottom diameter of the ring should be about 3¾" (95mm).

4. Glue the ripple edge pattern (page 183) to the top of the ring with repositionable adhesive.

5. Tilt the saw table to 40°, left side down, and cut along the inner line, cutting clockwise. Avoid cutting into the lower edge.

6. Tilt the table to 15°, left side down, and cut along the outer line, cutting clockwise.

7. Sand the inside and outside of the rippled ring, using an inflatable ball sander. You will complete the sanding later.

4 Glue the ripple edge pattern to the top ring.

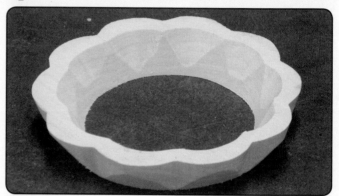

5,6 Cut the inner edge at 40° and the outer edge at 15°.

7 Sand the top ring.

Ripple-Edged Vase Pattern, neck
Copy at 100%

3 ½" (89mm)-diameter circle

TEST INCH

MAKING THE NECK

1. Place the neck pattern (opposite) on the piece of aspen saved from cutting ring 2 in Step 13 of Making the body. This will become one of the neck rings.

2. Cut out the circle at a 10° angle, saw table tilted left side down, cutting clockwise. Keep this piece wide side up and center the rippled top ring on top, keeping grains of both pieces aligned. It should overhang the neck slightly, and will be sanded down later.

3. Trace the inner circle of the rippled ring onto the neck.

4. Drill a slightly angled entry hole just inside the circle and cut

clockwise along the circle at 10°, saw table tilted left side down.

5. Place this ring, wide side up, on the 4" (102mm) piece of aspen, making sure to align the grains. Trace the inner and outer circles. Cut clockwise along these lines at 10°, saw table tilted left side down. This is the other neck ring.

6. Glue the two rings together, wide sides up, keeping the grains aligned. Clamp and let dry.

7. Sand the inside and outside smooth.

ASSEMBLING THE VASE

1. Invert ring set 2 so that the solid piece is on top.

2. Center the glued-up neck pieces, wide side up, on the solid piece of ring set 2, aligning grains. Trace the inside. This will form the opening of the vase. It should be about 2⅛" (54mm) in diameter.

3. Drill an entry hole at a 25° angle, facing the outside of the piece, on the circle you just traced. Cut along the circle at a 25° angle, saw table tilted left side down, cutting counterclockwise. You may need to cut a smaller circle first, with the table level, to allow clearance for the blade clamp.

4. Glue the rippled top ring to the wide face of the neck rings. Weight down and let dry. This forms the top assembly of the vase.

5. Finish shaping and smoothing the top assembly using the flexible pad and inflatable ball sanders. Round the lower edge of the rippled top ring where it meets the neck.

6. Glue center ring to ring set 2 (inverted set with hole). Clamp and let dry. Lightly sand the inside.

7. Glue this assembly to ring set 1 (straight set of glued-up rings and base). This completes the body of the vase. Weight down and let dry.

8. Lightly trace the outline of the top assembly on the vase body. Shape and sand the vase body, keeping the area inside the outline flat for gluing.

9. Glue the top assembly to the vase body. Weight down and let dry.

10. Do touch-up sanding as needed.

11. Finish with several coats of shellac, sanding between coats.

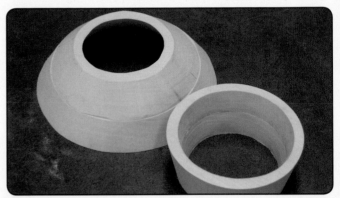
3 Cut the vase opening.

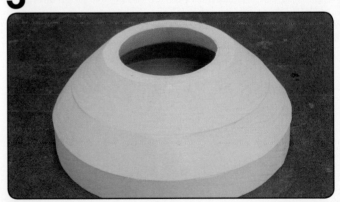
6 Glue center ring to ring set 2.

7 Glue ring set 2 to ring set 1.

RIPPLE-EDGED VASE

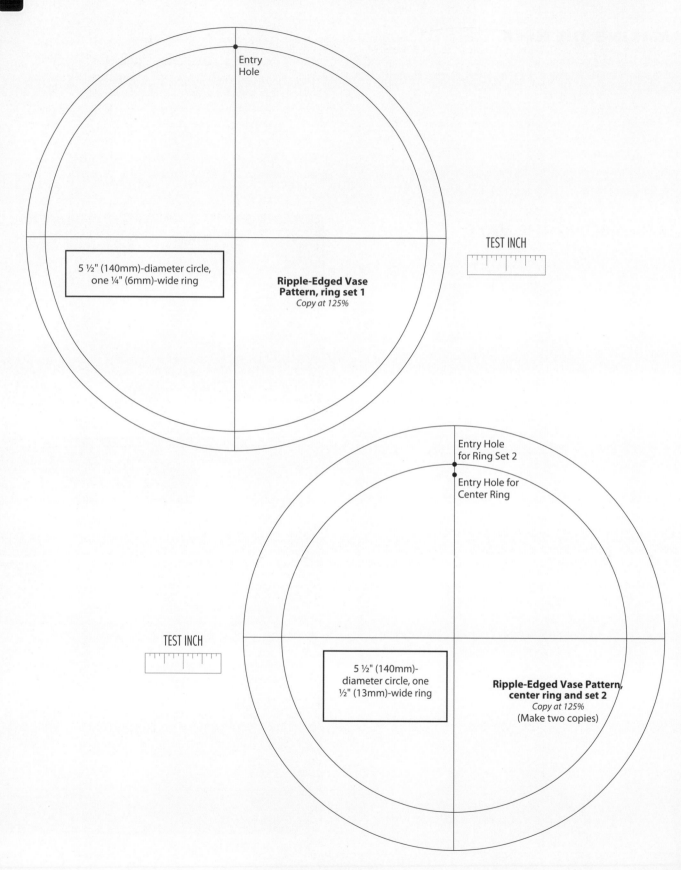

Entry
Hole

5 ½" (140mm)-diameter circle,
one ¼" (6mm)-wide ring

**Ripple-Edged Vase
Pattern, ring set 1**
Copy at 125%

TEST INCH

Entry Hole
for Ring Set 2

Entry Hole for
Center Ring

5 ½" (140mm)-
diameter circle, one
½" (13mm)-wide ring

**Ripple-Edged Vase Pattern,
center ring and set 2**
Copy at 125%
(Make two copies)

TEST INCH

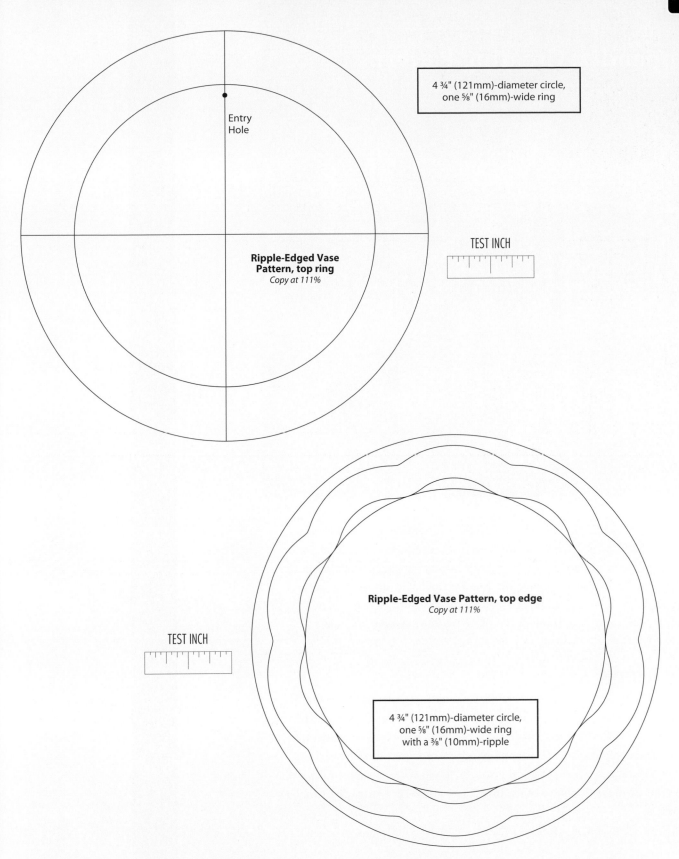

Entry
Hole

4 ¾" (121mm)-diameter circle,
one ⅝" (16mm)-wide ring

**Ripple-Edged Vase
Pattern, top ring**
Copy at 111%

TEST INCH

Ripple-Edged Vase Pattern, top edge
Copy at 111%

TEST INCH

4 ¾" (121mm)-diameter circle,
one ⅝" (16mm)-wide ring
with a ⅜" (10mm)-ripple

CHAPTER 6: Thinking Outside the Bowl

RIPPLE-EDGED VASE

Appendix: Creating Patterns

Did you ever have to buy wood for a project because what you had on hand was just a little too short, narrow, thick, or thin? Are you accumulating wonderful pieces of wood to use "one day"? By making your own patterns, or by adapting those from this book, you can use wood you already own, wood reclaimed from used furniture, or other people's castoffs. Here are some considerations to keep in mind as you move from my ideas to your own.

Patterns

Pattern making for bowls is quite straightforward, especially if you use the ring method, which requires drawing only an outline and one ring. Many of the patterns for this book were made with low-tech equipment, such as graph paper, ruler, compass, protractor, and a good eraser. Others were created with PolyDraw, a design tool for bowl makers, found at *scrollmania.com*. This powerful app makes it easy to generate precise patterns in an amazing variety of profiles.

Shapes and Sizes

When planning your bowl, keep in mind that contours become smaller with each successive ring. Be sure your bowl is sized so you can cut and sand the smallest ring. If your pattern is very intricate or the wood is hard to cut, try using fewer rings, or create wider curves and corners. Sometimes a simple circle is sufficient when a piece of wood is especially interesting.

Laminations

Laminations challenge your creativity and let you take your bowl to another level. They also use up wood left over from other projects. Here are a few tips to help you get the most from your laminations.

Color

To get a good idea of how your wood combinations will look when finished, wet the pieces of wood with mineral spirits or make a test application on scraps of wood with the finish you plan to use.

Be careful when sanding strongly colored wood like padauk, the dust of which can migrate into the pores of adjacent pieces. Try to sand from light to dark, when possible.

Try using a different color combination with the same lamination pattern. If you change ring width and cutting angle as well, you'll never know it was the same bowl.

Stripes and swags

Laminated strips that run through the center of the pattern (radial) will remain straight when cut and stacked. Laminated strips that go across the rings (tangential) will form swags. I did not include instructions in the book for the multicolor bowl shown above because I found that I could not align the swags precisely enough to prevent "jaggies." However, it is a clear example of how radial and tangential strips behave.

When tangential strips, seen in the back of this bowl, are used in a lamination design, swags are formed.

Ring Basics

No matter how simple or elaborate, a bowl is only as good as the rings it uses. These hints are good to keep in mind when you plan your bowls.

Entry holes

Always put entry holes in locations that are easy to sand, such as wide curves. Try not to have two entry holes back-to-back since that reduces the amount of wood available for sanding and shaping. This is most important for ¼" wide rings—wider rings are more forgiving.

Ring width

For any given wood thickness, narrower rings can take a smaller cutting angle than wider ones. This lets you cut bowls with more vertical sides. Wider rings are useful when you are working with wood that is dense or hard to control since there is more leeway for corrective shaping and sanding. Even wide rings can produce thin-sided bowls with enough aggressive sanding—see photo below.

This aspen bowl used rings that were ½" (13mm) wide, then sanded severely.

CREATING PATTERNS

Angles—The Final Word

For every combination of ring width and wood thickness there is a cutting angle that will result in rings that are nearly perfectly aligned. This angle is actually the smallest angle that will produce concentric rings from a single piece of wood. I call it the minimum cutting angle. If a smaller angle is used, the remaining piece of wood cannot be used for the next ring. If, however, a larger angle is used, the outer edge of the next ring can be trimmed, as is done when making bowls with curved sides.

The chart in Chapter One, page 16, gives minimum cutting angles for typical combinations of wood thickness and ring width. However, since not all wood is of standard thickness, it's useful to be able to determine the minimum cutting angle for any piece of wood. This angle is actually the amount that the saw table is moved from its normally level position, and is read on the scale under the saw table.

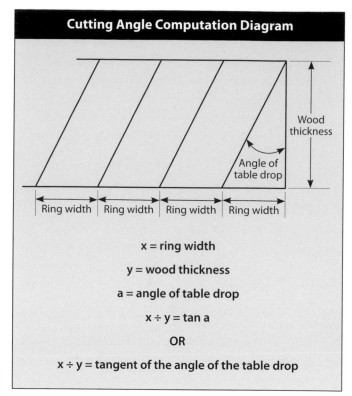

Cutting Angle Computation Diagram

Wood thickness

Angle of table drop

Ring width

x = ring width

y = wood thickness

a = angle of table drop

x ÷ y = tan a

OR

x ÷ y = tangent of the angle of the table drop

To find this angle, divide the ring width by the wood thickness and find the angle on the Cutting Angle Chart (below) that corresponds to your answer. For example, if your ring width is ⅜" (10mm) and your wood is ¾" (19mm) thick, divide ⅜" by ¾" (10mm by 19mm). Your answer will be 0.5. If you look at the cutting angle chart, you'll see that the closest number is .5095, which corresponds to a cutting angle of 27°. I like to increase the angle by one degree to provide an extra safety margin. This gives you a cutting angle of 28°. Use the same procedure for any thickness of wood and any ring width.

The cutting angle chart is really a tangent chart. You're actually computing the tangent of the cutting angle, which shows that you never know when your high school trigonometry will come in handy! See the Cutting Angle Computation Diagram (above) for an illustration of what you're computing, or just use the formula if you prefer. You can also go to *scrollmania.com* and use the Angle Calculator to compute the cutting angle. Whichever method you use, you'll be well equipped to figure out how to cut most any bowl successfully.

Cutting Angle Chart

Cutting Angle	Ring width ÷ wood thickness	Cutting Angle	Ring width ÷ wood thickness
15	0.2679	30	0.5773
16	0.2867	31	0.6008
17	0.3057	32	0.6248
18	0.3249	33	0.6493
19	0.3443	34	0.6744
20	0.3639	35	0.7001
21	0.3838	36	0.7265
22	0.4040	37	0.7535
23	0.4244	38	0.7812
24	0.4452	39	0.8097
25	0.4663	40	0.8390
26	0.4877	41	0.8692
27	0.5095	42	0.9003
28	0.5317	43	0.9324
29	0.5543	44	0.9656
		45	1.0000

Index

INDEX

About the Author

Carole Rothman, a psychologist, retired college professor, cake decorator, and woodworker, has been a craftsperson for most of her life. Her ongoing mission has been to integrate concepts and methods from diverse areas, then share her discoveries with others through writing and teaching.

A collapsible wooden basket, purchased at a craft fair many years ago, was the impetus for Carole to learn the scroll saw. Intrigued by how easily a flat piece of wood could be turned into a useful, three-dimensional object through angled cutting, she sought out similar projects. This led to the discovery of "bowls from a board," also known as "stacked ring bowls." Although some instructional material was available, it was typically quite rudimentary and the projects were not very appealing. Only one source offered guidance on making attractive, artistic bowls. However, the approach required the use of a router in addition to the scroll saw, and the instructions, which were devoid of explanation, were extremely difficult to follow. Nowhere to be found were comprehensive, systematic guidelines, or information on the principles underlying the process through which scroll saw and sanders alone were sufficient to produce striking bowls in a variety of profiles and configurations. Carole moved in to fill the void and, with the publication of *Wooden Bowls from the Scroll Saw*, created a new genre for scroll saw users. She continues her ongoing quest, to refine and expand the limits of this approach.

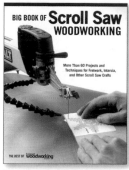
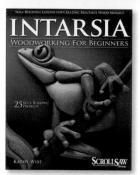
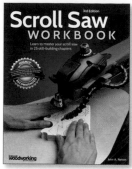
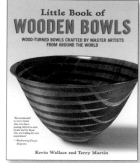
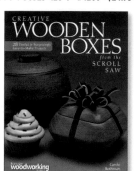
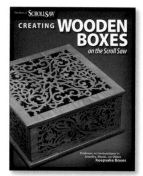
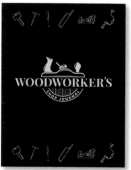